Losing
Susan

Losing Susan

BRAIN DISEASE,
THE PRIEST'S WIFE,
AND THE GOD WHO GIVES
AND TAKES AWAY

VICTOR LEE AUSTIN

BrazosPress
a division of Baker Publishing Group
Grand Rapids, Michigan

© 2016 by Victor Lee Austin

Published by Brazos Press
a division of Baker Publishing Group
P.O. Box 6287, Grand Rapids, MI 49516-6287
www.brazospress.com

Paperback edition published 2017
ISBN 978-1-58743-407-5

Printed in the United States of America

The Library of Congress has cataloged the hardcover edition as follows:
Names: Austin, Victor Lee, author.
Title: Losing Susan : brain disease, the priest's wife, and the God who gives and takes away / Victor Lee Austin.
Description: Grand Rapids : Brazos Press, 2016. | Includes bibliographical references.
Identifiers: LCCN 2015045179 | ISBN 9781587433856 (cloth)
Subjects: LCSH: Caregivers—Religious life. | Austin, Victor Lee. | Death—Religious aspects—Christianity. | Consolation. | Austin, Susan Lanier, 1955-1912. | Brain—Cancer—Patients—Biography
Classification: LCC BV4910.9 .A97 2016 | DDC 248.8/66092—dc23
LC record available at http://lccn.loc.gov/2015045179

17   18   19   20   21   22   23   7   6   5   4   3   2   1

In Memoriam
†
SUSAN LANIER AUSTIN

Born Susan Lanier Gavahan ∗ June 7, 1955
Las Vegas, New Mexico

Baptized ∗ September 4, 1955
Our Lady of Sorrows, Las Vegas

Confirmed ∗ December 8, 1974
Church of the Holy Faith, Santa Fe

Married Victor Lee ∗ September 29, 1978
Church of the Holy Faith

Gave birth to Michael Lee ∗ July 4, 1980
Santa Fe
and to Emily Parker ∗ July 3, 1984
Las Vegas

Died ∗ December 17, 2012
New York City

Requiem ∗ December 22, 2012
Saint Thomas Church Fifth Avenue

Contents

Body Knows—Blessed Speech Therapists—The Happy Return to October; Its Tragic End—The Best Book in the Bible—Sandy—What Is It?—The Kidneys Have Their Say—Crossing Another Line—Tears and Hope—December 17, 2012—May She Rest—A Christian Service—Little Lady—Why Have You Forsaken Me?—Divergence and a Dream

Preface

This is the story of an unusual woman. She was a wife, a mother, a Christian believer, a lover of children, a writer of stories, a foster mother to babies. She was nineteen years old when I first met her, thirty-eight years old when her brain tumor was diagnosed, fifty-seven years old when she died.

This is also my story, the story of an awkward boy who got to marry the first college girl to catch his eye, the story of a priest whose wife brought church truths home to the domestic reality of table and hearth, the story of a man who had to take increasing care of a woman whose mental state slowly declined over the last half of their marriage.

This is an unusual story, for the woman had unusual felicity with words and folk craft, and a heart with wise love for the good things for children. Unusual too, at least in the broader world, is to have a priest who is married; unusual, to be married to one spouse for thirty-four years; unusual, for the parties of the marriage to have entered it as virgins; and unusual, if trivial, for their home to have no television. This is not a story of statistically average people.

Yet for all that, it is, I have come to see, a universal story. Here was a woman who had much promise that was never fulfilled. But of whom can that not be said? Here was a man with hopes and projects for a theological career who found his life upended in order to care for the one to whom he had made a vow "for better for worse." But who has not known unexpected, forced life changes? Rare would be the readers who see nothing of themselves in this story.

There is more. It is a universal story also because, although but a slight chapter in the great history, this story has as its main character a very strange being who is involved with every chapter of any history. In the story before you, this strange character is silent on nearly every page, although he is never absent. I can testify that he was with me with tangible strength at some particular moments of absolute need. He never left me. I can also testify that, in this story, he gave me what my heart most desired—he gave me my wife.

But it must also be said that he is an awful character. I have found him to take away what he gives. He has led me into wild, frightful places, and I have sometimes wished that I had never made his acquaintance. And it remains true that I do not know him, not really.

This, you see, is a story with three characters. Two of us have names: Susan and Victor. And the third character is the one everyone calls God.

1

The Beginning

How We Met

I was valedictorian of my high school, which actually doesn't mean a lot—as exemplified by the fact that there was no tradition in my hometown of the valedictorian, notwithstanding the word, doing any speechifying at all, *vale* or otherwise. My town had ten thousand people in it, and we were the biggest thing for ninety miles. Think: cultural isolation. As a child with a strong intellectual bent, I had but a few friends, a small handful of people with whom there was a shared academic interest. Some of them were girls, but, alas, no girlfriends. Yet from early years I had a sense of the reality of God, of the importance of Bible stories, and of the importance of going to church.

So when I went to St. John's College in Santa Fe, it was with both excitement and fear. Excitement came from being within a small student body of about three hundred, all of whom were there to read the same books. Since St. John's had no electives, it would be okay there (and not at all weird) to talk at any time about the things we were studying. We would talk over meals about Socrates or whether it made any sense to think of a point as, according to Euclid's definition, "that which has no part." We would talk about Odysseus while we sat on benches in the high New Mexican sun. We would talk in our dorm rooms about Greek words and what it might mean for a language to be rather indifferent about word order. We would take walks and watch sunsets and talk about many important things. This had never happened to me before. It was like being on drugs, without the chemicals. (Not that, innocent me, I knew anything about drugs.) Our minds were alive: excitement.

But I also came to St. John's with fear. What if, once I moved into this lively intellectual world, I found that Christian faith could not stand up to reason's scrutiny? Questions would be asked, and I might find no answers for them. Would I survive rigorous challenge to my faith?

So when I saw posted an announcement for a Bible study on Saturday morning, I eagerly went to the little common room where the group met, a half-dozen people as I recall. I don't remember what we studied that morning, nor can I positively recall that the group continued to meet thereafter. What was important to me occurred at the end of that meeting. I asked if anyone was going to church tomorrow.

A blonde junior girl said, "I am, but it's Episcopal."

"I don't care," I answered. At the time, I was a Presbyterian but without particularly strong ties to the denomination; my Christianity had been a matter of a sort of generic small-town evangelicalism. For the most part, I was innocent of theological difference, basically seeing the only important question as whether one was a Christian or not.

Now I hear that odd answer—"but it's Episcopal"—as providential irony. God was going to draw me into a form of catholic religion through this junior with long, straight, blonde hair.

How We Went to Church

Susan (of course it was she) told me to meet her outside the dining hall at nine o'clock on Sunday and that we'd walk to church. This was new to me. Walking to church? It would take almost an hour to get there—the service was at ten—and then we would walk back and return to school in time for lunch. We'd miss breakfast, and we'd walk some five miles altogether (the return would be the uphill half, for the school was nestled up at the foot of Monte Sol and the church, Holy Faith, was literally downtown). We'd walk streets that were strange to me, a boy brought up in a town where everything was on a grid. Santa Fe streets in the 1970s (as, to a lesser extent, they remain today) were windy, barely paved, going past stucco walls and houses and galleries and restaurants that were hardly set back at all. Nothing here was ordinary to me. I had journeyed to a new world.

Dear reader, if you want to get to know someone well, try walking to church with her week in and week out. Make it a long walk, so that it takes the whole morning. When people stop to offer you a ride, wave them off with a friendly smile. Tell them, "We want to walk"; that's what Susan and I would say.

Before long I was saturated with love for this new being. We had conversations at other times during the week. Being older, she knew a lot more than I about the Great Books. She also knew a lot of old folk songs. We went to waltz parties together and (amazingly on my part) won the waltz contest at the Fasching ball that fall. The prize was a dinner for two at a restaurant called the Compound.

I started to get to know her friends.

That Summer

One of Susan's friends was named Mary. (Yes, for my Catholic readers, *that* Mary.) I didn't know anything about her. While on a trip to New Mexico during high school, my church's youth group had stepped into a chapel. Afterwards I asked our minister about the statues. He told me that one of them was Mary, and that unfortunately Catholics sometimes put too much emphasis upon her. The important person for us Presbyterians was Jesus.

For Susan, there was not only Jesus; there was also Mary. Susan wrote me a few letters over the following summer, bulging fat envelopes with several half sheets covered in her small hand. She instructed me in how to say the rosary. She gave me the words for the Angelus. She copied hymns for me, listed the spiritual gifts, and wrote out a number of other traditional Catholic devotions. She wrote also about her love for God, her desire to be a priest, her questions about becoming Roman Catholic or Orthodox. She wrote about the monastic vows and whether it was better to be celibate or married. She would mention how she had been able to go to church on a Sunday, or not; she didn't drive back then, so whether she went to church depended on others in her family, others who didn't quite see the point of it but might be persuaded on her account.

The Previous Christmas

Susan had had a boyfriend during her first two years at St. John's. I learned that he had moved into her room, but that they had not, shall we say, consummated relations. This was considered unusual for him; there was something about Susan that solicited what in a more gallant age would have been called respect. He too was witty and brilliant, and was in addition strongly athletic. (Yes, when I learned of him, I was jealous.) But after two years, he had had enough of St. John's, so by the time I arrived he was not on the scene.

Their arrangement upon parting was for Susan to visit him at his parents' home at Christmas (which turned out to be the first Christmas after I met her). So she did, and the two of them went to midnight mass at an Episcopal cathedral. Afterwards, he asked her to marry him.

She told me this about a month later. I held my breath. She had declined.

Her Brilliant Childhood

Susan taught herself how to read and, indeed, liked to relate that she invented multiplication by herself one day while lying on her bed, some time before she entered school. Her mother took her to the public education authorities and persuaded them to let her skip first grade. With a summer birthday, that meant she was barely six when she started school (second grade), and she was barely seventeen when she started St. John's. She graduated at the age of twenty. Her classmates recall a promise she made to her mother, that she wouldn't drink until she was twenty-one—which meant that, being true to her word, she stood out as a non-imbiber at many college parties.

I often resented her having skipped first grade. She was in fact just nine months older than I, but here I had come on the scene unnecessarily late in her life. If only she had been but a sophomore when I arrived at college! Then I would have had more time to be with her.

A Hug

I loved to visit Susan's room to talk about God and books and generally about everything, as is the way with Johnnies (St. John's students). One such visit ended with a hug—I have no idea how it ended with something so longed-for but unhoped-for—and then I became a bit embarrassed when I realized I was aroused. She said nothing; I said nothing; but months later she mentioned that she had felt it.

At another time she invited me to give her a backrub. In the course of it, she asked me to put my hands under her shirt on her skin. I muttered some hesitation, to which she said with exasperation: "I'm lying facedown!" So, with cheerful obedience and trepid joy, my hands rubbed her back. I noted silently that my months-long conjecture was true, that she wore no bra.

Reader, you may think I was unbelievably young and insufferably hung up about things physical. You are likely right. But I was indeed drawn to God and to Susan at the same time. Drawn to God, I held the traditional Christian belief that sexual relations were reserved by his design for marriage. All that this meant to me at the time was the negative prohibition of sex prior to and in any way outside of marriage. I did not know the goodness of the human body; I knew only that it could be easily misused. But as I was drawn to Susan, I was discovering the goodness of a body. What made it wonderful—and indeed, I think it was the unknown heart of her attraction—was that in being drawn to Susan I was discovering the unified physical and spiritual goodness of a person who was herself most drawn to God.

The Second-Best Book in the Bible

There is a clue to the union of human and divine love in the Bible itself, but it's in a book that I had never paid attention to. In this I was unlike, say, Garrison Keillor, the inventor of Lake Wobegon, who tells (at least in my memory) of being a boy sitting in church, bored. When this happened (and it was not infrequent), he would pick up the Bible and make a pretense of turning to the Psalms. But he was really aiming at the Song of Songs.

Let's look at this little book. It is entirely about the erotic longing of a bride and a groom for each other. It opens with desire, boldly stated: "May he smother me with kisses" (1:2). Throughout we find vivid love-making language. The bride says, for example,

"My beloved is for me a sachet of myrrh lying between my breasts" (1:13), while the bridegroom answers, "How beautiful you are, my dearest, ah, how beautiful, your eyes are like doves! . . . Our couch is shaded with branches" (1:15–16). The lovers are not bashful about describing each other's body. The groom speaks to his bride: "How beautiful you are, my dearest, how beautiful! Your eyes are doves behind your veil, your hair like a flock of goats streaming down Mount Gilead. Your teeth are like a flock of ewes newly shorn. . . . Your lips are like a scarlet thread, and your mouth is lovely; your parted lips. . . . Your neck. . . . Your two breasts are like two fawns, twin fawns of a gazelle grazing among the lilies" (4:1–5). Then she speaks of him: "My beloved is fair and desirable. . . . His head is gold, finest gold. His locks are like palm-fronds, black as the raven. His eyes are like doves beside pools of water. . . . His cheeks are like beds of spices, terraces full of perfumes; his lips are lilies, they drop liquid myrrh. His arms are golden rods set with topaz, his belly a plaque of ivory adorned with sapphires. His legs are pillars of marble set on bases of finest gold; his aspect is like Lebanon, noble as cedars. His mouth is sweetness itself, wholly desirable" (5:10–16). Although these speech-figures are not in every instance the sort of thing we might say to someone we love—has any boy you know ever told a girl that her teeth are "a flock of ewes"?—still the romantic import is clear. The poetry is in service of human erotic passion. It is bold, unashamed, and frank.

Not only bored boys in church wonder what the Song of Songs is doing in the Bible. Saints and scholars have wondered too. To begin with: Why doesn't the book ever mention God? He seems absent, the book entirely a collection of love poems of a man and a woman for each other. And what is going on in the book? We find a wee bit of drama. He comes to the door; she is slow to answer; when she opens, he is not there. They are separated; they find each other. She runs to look for him; he is looking for her; and so forth. But the book lacks an overall plot. There are also textual questions: Who is speaking? Some of the lines are clearly in the voice of one or the other person, but others are not. If you compare contemporary translations, you will find particular verses ascribed variously.

In sum, the problematic is that God is not mentioned, some of the metaphors are culturally odd, and the principle of organization is not clear, while nonetheless the passion and the beauty of the Song come through. What sense are we to make of these sexy poems as part of Holy Scripture?

One answer—and I think it is a true answer, if not the whole truth—is that the poems of the Song of Songs are allegorical poems that speak of the love between God and Israel, which by extension we may take to be the love between God and the church. Although contemporary biblical scholars tend to view allegorical interpretations as external impositions upon a biblical text, which therefore ought to be eschewed, it seems likely to me that *the original intent* of the text is for some such allegory to be read. We could say, for example, that God comes knocking for Israel to open up her home and receive him, but she is slow to respond, and when she does respond, it is too late. This could be read as a commentary on the period of the kings, which ends with the exile to Babylon; it is furthermore, as Robert Jenson says, "a pattern of Israel's history as the prophets sometimes proclaimed it." Indeed, Jenson shows that this intended allegory makes sense of many of the poems in this book that otherwise lack narrative coherence.

Yet for our purposes here we need not dig so deep. We could answer that the Song of Songs is nestled amongst the books of the Bible *in order that we will not think of erotic human love as essentially antithetical to holiness*. That is to say, it might not be that the Song of Songs gives us an answer so much as it gives us a question; or rather, it answers a simple question and thereby raises a larger one. If the question is, "Can the erotic love of a man and a woman be holy?" then the Song, just by its presence within what is called Holy Writ, says yes. The Song vividly makes the claim that there need be no antithesis between human and divine love. Yet it makes that claim without explaining it. We know, through painful experience, that a lot of human love runs contrary to God. A lot of human love is wayward, inconstant, and even adulterous, leading sometimes to physical violence and mental cruelty and a multitude of social ills. The Song of Songs tells us it need not be so. It says to us that somehow—even when we know not how—these two loves are intertwined with one another. And thereby it leaves us with the question.

Because human love can so easily be ungodly, should we fear it? Should we surround it with fences? Should we understand it in terms of negative prohibitions? As a boy, I had learned that sex outside of marriage was bad. And that knowledge, I am sure, saved me from many misfortunes.

But then, here came Susan into my life. Here was a person who was herself full of God's love who at the same time filled me with erotic love. I was loving her and God at once. I was not loving her as a means to God; I was longing for her precisely in her flesh as she was. And at the same time, through and with her my love for God was also newly aroused. I was being drawn closer to her and closer to God at once; and I had never before had any idea that such attractions could happen together, with each other.

I suppose I had never tried to understand the Song of Songs. Nowadays—on the far side of my marriage to Susan—I like to call it the second-best book in the Bible (the title of "best book" being reserved for more painful things to come). The Song puts the fully erotic passion of bride and groom in the midst of the sacred things. From within that wonder we ask, *how can this be?*

Rejection and Reversal

After her graduation Susan moved out of state to help an older sister with child care, but by the beginning of my senior year she had returned to Santa Fe and was living downtown with a couple of former Johnnies. She had landed a job as a bookkeeper for a glass company whose manager was also a Johnnie. So I got to see her often, spending many Sundays (afternoons as well as mornings) with her.

My interest in marrying her must have become obvious during that year. I remember talking about it once as we sat in my little Audi Fox. She held my hand and, stroking my palm, noted how it had no callouses. I was a skinny guy with near-zero athletic aptitude, and I didn't know anything about working with my hands. In other words: nice mind, maybe even nice soul, but not a body she was drawn to marry.

Sadness. I compared myself to T. S. Eliot's Prufrock, who sees and hears lovely beings singing and is almost carried away—and then reality cuts in: "I do not think that they will sing to me." During spring break of my senior year, not knowing what to do, I visited Nick, an old high school friend in Oklahoma, and persuaded him to move with me to Santa Fe. He came out to my graduation, and we found a couple of rooms to rent; then at the end of the month he drove with me from Oklahoma to Santa Fe. That was May 31, 1978, which on the church calendar is the feast of the Visitation of Mary to Elizabeth.

By prearrangement, I left Nick at our rooms and visited Susan at the glass shop, taking her for a hamburger after work. Sometime that evening, perhaps in the restaurant, perhaps afterwards as we sat in the car parked at her apartment, she took my uncalloused hand and said, "I've decided to accept your offer of marriage."

I couldn't believe it. It was as if all the lights in the universe had gone dark and then come back on, all new, just for me.

For years later, whenever I told this story I maintained that my first response was somehow to suppress the question, "What offer of marriage?" But in telling the story that way, I had in fact blotted out of memory her earlier rejection—something Nick has since been able to bring back to my mind. The truth is that I didn't understand my offer of marriage to be still "on the table." But of course it was, as she knew.

My summer plans were immediately upended. I had previously arranged to spend the month of June as a guest at the austere Monastery of Christ in the Desert; instead, that got cut back to just over a week. And Nick's plans too would be changed. I returned to our rooms late in the evening of that May 31 and told him that I had drawn him out to Santa Fe only to abandon him: that Susan would be marrying me.

Susan and I saw no reason to delay marriage—and we were not going to move in together beforehand. Since there were many important people in our lives named Michael (a priest at the monastery; my brother; and a personally influential Russian Orthodox priest and St. John's tutor, Michael Ossorgin), we chose to marry on September 29, the feast of Saint Michael and All Angels.

Susan wrote to her parents. The report we heard was that her mother read the letter and immediately, taking a bottle of Harvey's Bristol Cream sherry, retired to her bedroom and closed the door. I wrote to my parents, who still have my letter. No permissions were asked. We went to the Church of the Holy Faith and said we wanted to be married there on the evening of Friday, September 29. Father Campbell was pleased. With his permission, we asked the rector of the other Episcopal church in town also to be part of the wedding. He grinned and turned to me: "What took you so long, Victor?" Little did he know that the delay wasn't mine.

And so it happened that I was married after much longing, and what seemed to me like interminable waiting, to the dream of my eyes: a beautiful, thin, unusual, God-loving friend of Mary who was intellectually brilliant and a continual surprise to me. I was exactly twenty-two and a half years old when we were married. Susan was a bit over twenty-three. It would be fifteen years before her tumor was found.

Heart's Desire

The words "heart's desire" occur four times in the Psalter of the
(1979 U.S.) Book of Common Prayer. We find them first used of
the wicked who boast of their ungodly persecution of the poor.
"The wicked boast," says the psalmist, "of their heart's desire"
(10:3). But God will not let the wicked prevail, and in three other
instances, the reader of the Psalms is assured that God does grant
the desire of the heart. Consider Psalm 20, which is a prayer that
one can imagine being sung around a table on the evening that
begins the Sabbath:

> May the Lord answer you in the day of trouble,
> the Name of the God of Jacob defend you;
> Send you help from his holy place
> and strengthen you out of Zion;
> Remember all your offerings
> and accept your burnt sacrifice;
> Grant you your heart's desire
> and prosper all your plans.
>
> (20:1–4)

Here is the request that God grant "your heart's desire," the
desire of the heart of the one to whom the psalmist or the reader
is speaking. In the following psalm, the reader declares to God
that God has fulfilled this promise for the king (whom we may
understand to be David or some subsequent king also after the
Lord's heart): "You have given him his heart's desire" (21:2).

But it is Psalm 37 that has spoken most strongly to me. It has
a dynamic reflexivity: when you read this psalm you are reading
words that are spoken to you, the reader. As I read Psalm 37,
the psalmist tells me with the familiarity of my own voice not
to be anxious, not to fret over the conditions of the world, not
to despair when it seems that wickedness and lies are carrying
the day:

> Do not fret yourself because of evildoers;
> do not be jealous of those who do wrong.
> For they shall soon wither like the grass,
> and like the green grass fade away.
> Put your trust in the LORD and do good;
> dwell in the land and feed on its riches.
> Take delight in the LORD,
> and he shall give you your heart's desire.
>
> (37:1–4)

There it is, the promise: God gives to those who trust him what their hearts most desire. I look back to that college boy from Oklahoma and I see that this is concretely true. God gave me my heart's desire. It's God's nature to do so, and we can trust him to fulfill this promise.

What I didn't then know was that, having given me my heart's desire, God would proceed to take it away.

The Advent Calendar

So we were married; we had a son; we moved to New York City for seminary; we had a daughter; I became a priest. The things that drew me to Susan manifested themselves in new ways through these changes.

The children of clergy suffer a particular danger of growing up without faith. This is not, as is often thought, because they grow up too close to the inner workings of the church and thus are repelled by its darker, institutional sides. It's worse than that. Clergy children grow up intimately near to a human being—in my case, their father—who is supposed to be a real Christian, who of all people really ought to be exemplifying the ideals of Christianity day to day. Parishioners can be kept at a distance from the foibles and failures of their religious leaders. But the children of the clergy: they are there when the door is closed and the clerical collar is removed.

Yet disillusionment with and rebellion from Christian faith did not occur with our children. A signal reason for this is that Susan's faith was woven through everything she was. She didn't leave the Christian religion behind when she exited the doors of the church; she brought it with her into our home. Until the post–brain tumor decline set in, which is to say for a bit more than the first decade of our children's lives, Susan was continually adapting and creating home rituals.

One that I still use, even in my widowhood, is an Advent calendar she constructed when we were in seminary. It is adapted from the idea of a Jesse tree. She made twenty-four cards out of the blank side of the heavy cover of a package of watercolor paper. (With her father an environmentalist, Susan was a recycler before it was trendy to be one.) Each card has a tiny hole in the top, through which a string runs. There is a purple cloth into which she sewed loops; onto those loops the cards are tied, one per day starting with December 1. Over the first eighteen days the cards make a rectangular frame, working from the bottom up both sides to meet in the center of the top. Each of these cards shows an ancestor of Jesus; all together they tell the story of preparation, from Adam and Eve up to Mary. The final six cards, which are larger, form a tableau in the middle: shepherds, angels, palm trees, and animals, with the baby in a cradle for December 24.

Susan used origami paper for the illustrations on the cards. They are winsome pictures. Adam holds a dog. Eve faces a tree out of which a snake hangs. Leah has her hands over her eyes. Mary stands, a small figure with her back to us, facing an expanse of gold (Susan's way of showing the Annunciation).

Every year we hung the cloth, and then, each evening, one of us would tell the story of the day and hang up the appropriate card. As the children grew, they were invited to tell the story. And as they got older, we would embellish the tale.

"Jacob wanted to marry Rachel, who was very beautiful. So he worked seven years. He didn't like Rachel's sister, Leah, because

Leah had bad eyes. You'll see here she's covering her eyes. She thinks she's ugly, and Jacob thought that too. She probably would have looked a lot prettier if she'd had eyeglasses, but they didn't have eyeglasses back then. They didn't even have eye doctors. There were a lot of other things they didn't have, like telephones and automobiles and hot cross buns. That's just how it was.

"Well, at the end of the seven years, Rachel's father made a switcheroo on Jacob. He gave him Leah as his wife, rather than Rachel. In those days not only did they not have eyeglasses; they didn't have electricity. In fact, there weren't even flashlights. I don't think they had matches. So Jacob got married in the dark and didn't know who it was that he married. But the next morning he saw: it was Leah.

"As you can imagine, he was pretty mad, but Rachel's father said, 'Don't be angry. You can have Rachel too—just work another seven years.' So Jacob married Rachel also and worked a lot longer for his father-in-law. It's not easy having two wives. Between them and their handmaids, Jacob had twelve sons. One of them was Judah. We'll talk about him tomorrow. But what we note today is that Judah was a son of Leah. And that's why Leah's on our calendar."

I'd try to string out the story as long as I could—goading our children, Michael and Emily, to join me and make it even longer—but Susan would bring us back to the task. For there wasn't just her Advent calendar. There was also the Advent wreath on the dining table, and there was the Metropolitan Museum of Art Christmas Tree Advent Calendar, and there were lots more Advent calendars (because she could never throw away any calendar; we'd just get another and use them all). And closer to Christmas there were the crèches that had to be put up and, day by day, added to. It took a lot of time.

This was her genius: to create domestic rituals in which Christian faith became a home reality. We looked forward to them, even as they multiplied, and even when we had Other Things To

Do, things like homework or evening church meetings. We still did the Advent calendar.

When, over the years, Susan's energy abated and her brain slowed, we continued to put up her Advent calendar. As I mentioned, I still put it up.

The Tree of Life

How is it that a child comes to know that God is real, that the Bible stories are important for the child's own life, that what happens in a church is significant outside its doors? How is it that a child comes to talk to God? Every possible answer falls short. If we say it's because of the faith of the parents, that can't be enough, because sometimes one child will know God as real and another will be largely insensitive. If we say it's because the child has read the Bible stories, the same objection applies. If we say it's because of Sunday school teachers, or the worship of the church, or anything else done by other people, we still have the same objection. Nor can we say it's because of the child's own exploration and study. Some children read the Bible and think about God and know in their hearts that God is a real presence to them, while other children read and think and know nothing of the sort.

Nonetheless, there is something wonderful about living as if there were no question at all about our faith. Susan was able to create such an environment. She made Christian faith real in multiple facets of our family life, using not only Bible stories but the calendar of the Christian year with its feasts and fasts, the stories of the saints, and stories of her own writing that she shared with our children. Our family custom was to sing Christmas carols on Thanksgiving Day, in order not to sing them during Advent, in order to build up to the joy of celebrating Jesus' birth. We had special foods for various seasons, but especially for Easter, for which Susan made pascha and kulich (traditional Russian sweet molded cheese and bread). At the beginning of our marriage she had taught herself how to make Ukrainian Easter eggs, and over the years she initiated our children into their complexities during the long weeks of Lent.

To me it is a marvel that, when Susan's ability to be an active mother for our children diminished as we felt the encroaching effects of her brain disease, our children did not lose their faith. They might well have. They might have said, "Any God who takes away a lovely Mama like mine is not a God I will love." That they didn't—that their faith perdured and grew—is the fruition of the seeds Susan had planted since their birth.

And yet, despite all this, there is mystery. It might have turned out differently. Towards the beginning of Terrence Malick's film *The Tree of Life*, we see a few scenes from the childhood of the woman who has learned that one of her sons has died. The film puts us with this mother as she thinks back to her girlhood, and her adult voice whispers, offscreen, a barely discernible question, "When did I first know you?" I think that is just the way prayer is: a voice whispered, oblique, offscreen. I also think that this particular question is a perfect question even as it is unanswerable. When was it that any of us who know God first knew him? And how can we know God, since he is in our lives always "offscreen"? As far as I am able to think back, he seems to have been there before me, and in my memory I see him with me. I am a boy in church not yet four years old, and I know he is real. I am walking through a pasture in Oklahoma, and I know he is all around.

It is clear to me, as I write this, that Susan's invention of that Advent calendar was a working of God's grace, a piece of the work he was doing in and for her and for me and our children and the many people we have shared it with. But it is unclear, in fact completely unknowable, how this grace of God works. I come to the edge of the mystery of God's providence, and of free will, and I have nothing to say.

Christmas Day

Probably no day of the year is more altered for clergy children than Christmas Day. I remember my own childhood Christmases: waking up on my grandparents' Oklahoma farm, running into the living room and seeing for the first time all the presents wrapped and stuffed as near the tree as they could be. My brother and I would awaken our parents, and soon everyone was sitting around in pajamas and the presents would be opened. Opening presents was the most important thing of the day, and it took absolute precedence over everything else, including getting dressed and having breakfast!

But for a priest, even when the Christmas Eve service is the most splendid liturgy for the feast, there will be a service on Christmas Day also, a service offered particularly for those who cannot be out in the middle of the night for the midnight mass. So a clergy family has to do things differently. Here's how it worked out when I was rector of the Church of the Resurrection in Dutchess County, New York.

We had a pull-out-all-the-stops midnight mass from which we'd be home by about one in the morning. The children went to bed while Susan and I finished wrapping presents and placing them under the tree. We consumed the milk and cookies that the children had left out for Santa. (This was an old family tradition on Susan's side. Her father had once left a note: "Thanks for the cookies. Dancer has strong teeth. [Signed] Santa.") We went to bed and slept for a few hours.

When the children awoke, they knew there would be stockings, and they could get us up and get the goodies therein: usually a small toy, a puzzle, a piece of fruit, some nuts and candy, and a coin. But then they had to wait.

Susan made cinnamon rolls from scratch using a family recipe. On the day before Christmas she would have made the dough and then let it rest, covered, in the refrigerator overnight. Now on Christmas morning, perhaps with some child labor thrown in, the rolls were finished and baked. Out from the oven came our smell of Christmas. She also cooked "little smokies" and scrambled eggs. We had a breakfast satisfying to nose, palate, and stomach.

And then I left them and went to church, and again they had to wait. I'd be back home about eleven o'clock, at which time, at last, the presents could be opened!

After presents, Susan got the Christmas dinner going. One year we had a goose, as I recall; she did a crown roast at least twice; we often had Yorkshire pudding. And lots and lots of other food, including multiple pies and many sweet things. While dinner was cooking, the children had time to play with their new toys. Susan and I might have started reading a new book. And I'm sure, after the great meal, we took a walk and a nap, although perhaps not in that order.

Michael and Emily remember the magic of these Christmases. I see them as a signal instance of Susan combining her love of God, her love of children, her delight in the Christian year, all with her desire to "bring it home."

In this way also, church and family fit together.

A few years after her brain surgery and treatments, we were still living as if everything had been cured and all was back to normal. And then there came that year's Christmas afternoon. The dinner's ingredients were all in the refrigerator. I had come home from church, and the presents were now all opened. And we watched Susan go to her bedroom to take a nap. She didn't say anything. She didn't ask us to take over. She just got up from the living room and went to bed. I looked at Michael and Emily, both teenagers now, and realized that if we were going to have Christmas dinner, we would be cooking it ourselves. Which we were glad to do, of course; but something had changed. Something had just slipped away from us.

We were on the edge of a strange land, and we had no idea what was ahead.

A Letter to Mr. Buckley

Before going on with this story, I need to give you examples of how passionately Susan could write. The first is a letter that arose from the conjunction of three things: her love of children, her experience with boats, and my reading habits. She got her love of boats from her mother, who, although she had to raise her daughters in the dry heights of northern New Mexico, nonetheless managed to teach them sailing on a local irrigation lake. They sailed small pram boats, some of which her mother had made herself. They also frequently summered on Cape Cod with a grandmother who lived on a pond that opened into the sea. From my reading, Susan was introduced to *National Review* and, more particularly, to the books by its editor, William F. Buckley Jr., especially *Airborne*, Buckley's account of sailing across the Atlantic. She wrote this letter in the fall of 1980:

> *Dear Mr. Buckley,*
>
> *On the night of the debate between Reagan and Anderson, my husband and I, to our surprise, came close to a quarrel. The efficient (but not final) cause lay in the question of whether or not the way people think ought to be allowed to influence the way they vote (Mr. Anderson referred to this as the issue of the separation of church and state). By certain well-trodden paths our discussion of this came to center on abortion, my husband more than ordinarily desperate, and I (this being the source of the near-quarrel) most unusually perverse. To his cries that those who call abortion a matter of private choice simply are not rational, I would reply, "Aha, but suppose you were the one with ten children and a*

drunken husband, faced with carrying this weight for nine months." An impasse.

The ultimate cause of my perversity was Michael, my first born son, who was brought forth and wrapped in swaddling clothes on the Fourth of July of this very year. I do not say that I brought him forth, because he was delivered by Caesarean section. On the other hand I did carry him for many months, past the time (6 months) when everyone I met asked me if I would be going to the hospital that afternoon, past the time (8 months) when everyone I met asked me if I was sure it wasn't twins, right up to the time (9 months and 4 days) when everyone I met gasped in horror that someone who looked like I did should actually be walking around. Furthermore I labored with him for 36 hours before they finally put us under. A sufficiently vivid experience to concentrate the mind wonderfully.

Now that I know what I think, I have concluded that the Supreme Court justices were not fools, or not perfect fools, when they related abortion with a woman's right to privacy. Merely to carry a child is to have your privacy invaded, not now and then, but at every moment of the nine months, and inescapably. To what room can you go to stop the child inside from tickling when he first begins to move? How can you avoid him in the shower, at church, at prayer in your dark bedroom? Everywhere he interrupts, cries without sound, distracts, tugs at you, and, most dreadfully, lives—is alive—inside your own body. What if your arm came to life and, taking blood and strength still from your heart, found its own activities and thoughts were sufficient for it, without regard to yours? It is almost unbearably startling (never mind that you have expected it for a month) to feel your child quicken in your womb.

It is not, as the heretics say, that the conceived thing has no personhood till he is born, but rather that he has too

*much. His personality is intense and frightening. If, as they
say, a woman has the right to do what she likes with her own
body, all they can mean is that she can do her best to eject
this small stranger who will not leave except by violence.
Their inconsistency is to say that the conceptus is a mere
thing, a germ. It is not things but persons whose existences
impinge so on our own.*

*This being so I can readily see that the invasion might be
insupportable to a woman, and the temptation strong to lay
hands on the invader. Insupportable, yes, but not—with one
eye on the beautiful face of our Michael—not indefensible.
Amen, Lord Jesus. Come quickly.*

*Late that night I woke my husband up. "I have the solu-
tion to the abortion controversy," I said.*

"What?" he said patiently.

*"When two people have strong and conflicting claims
where do they go to be resolved?"*

"To court."

*Let a woman take her unborn child to court and, in front
of twelve good men and true, accuse him of placing on her
an impossible burden physical or emotional. Let the court
appoint him an attorney for his defense and give him what
he has always lacked—a say in the matter of his own life
and death.*

*She will not have the right to do what she likes with her
own body, since she will be prevented from doing what she
likes with his. But she will be allowed to free herself from
impossible situations and her case will be judged on its mer-
its—which is surely how it ought to be judged. And the babies
will have a voice, which perhaps will quiet their soundless
protest which drives my husband to desperation.*

*His only comment on my brilliant solution was that I
should write and let you know about it. "Reagan," he said,
"gets all his ideas from Buckley." The assumption is that*

Reagan, *as our next president, will take care of passing the necessary laws to put it into effect. If the Supreme Court gets uppity about it, Congress could deny it appellate jurisdiction (ex parte McCardle). The fireworks would be marvelous.*

Very truly yours,
Susan Austin

P.S. Michael still has to nurse in the middle of the night, and to keep myself from falling asleep and dropping him off the bed, I need a good supply of very gripping books. Victor's contribution to the cause was Airborne, *which has turned out to be one of the rare ones that grips so hard that I keep on reading long after he has fallen back to sleep. This letter comes to you with admiration and gratitude.*

The great man wrote back to her as follows:

October 8, 1980

Dear Mrs. Austin:
   That is a charming and bright letter, for which I thank you. You have a most ingenious thought, marvelously presented, and I am taking the liberty of sending your letter to the editor and publisher of the Human Life Review, *my friend and colleague James McFadden (though I have nothing to do with his enterprise). I am so pleased a) that you thought to write to me, and b) that you did so with such charming informality and c) that you liked my sailing book. With all good wishes,*

Yours faithfully,
Wm. F. Buckley, Jr.

As a result of this, J. P. McFadden started a correspondence with Susan, which led in a few months' time to Susan writing for him a critique of the popular feminist self-care book *Our Bodies, Ourselves*. This was published in 1981, with him introducing Susan as "a new talent." She had signed her essay "Susan Lanier Austin," but Mr. McFadden advised her to be just "Susan Austin." "Someday you'll thank me," he said.

Susan Is Published on Abortion

It was in 1982 that we moved to New York City for seminary. Only I was in the program of study for the priesthood. Susan had come to discern that her calling was elsewhere: in motherhood, in making our home Christian, and in writing.

We found many things about New York harsh for us. The city had much dirt and graffiti, the subways were loud and hot (or cold), and everything was expensive. There were no Starbucks then—I know it's unsophisticated to like Starbucks, but I remember when there was no place in the city to go in and sit down and no bathroom to use. We were living on a shoestring, and a treat was to buy a sausage from a street vendor (and to eat it standing up).

The first gracious thing that happened to us was an invitation from Mr. McFadden (who asked us to call him "Jim"). We had been in the city only a few weeks when he invited us to join him at the now-closed Paone's on East Thirty-Fourth Street. Over lunch, he fixed his eyes on Susan: "When did you learn to write?" He loved her prose. Susan, of course, had been writing from the first day she could hold a pencil. She was reading by the age of four and had soaked up everything she read (along with some above-average teaching in a few public school classes). Jim went on to invite us to his home for his semiannual open houses: on the day of the Steuben parade, in honor of his German heritage, and on Saint Patrick's, in honor of his Irish. His hospitality was gracious and ecumenical and open-armed; in a hostile world, in a harsh city, at a difficult time, Jim's humane virtues provided for us a haven of peace.

Nearly three decades later—as it happened, in a providential lull in the midst of her final illness—the current editors of the *Review* reprinted the second article of Susan's that Jim had published. Although she was no longer in a state to write such a thing, and in fact could not remember ever having been able to write as she did in that piece, upon reading it Susan radiated joy. I showed it to several people at Saint Thomas Church (our current parish) who had never known the earlier Susan. They were, every one, amazed and moved. No one who knew gentle Susan—a frail woman who found it hard to carry on a conversation but easy to smile—no one could believe she had ever written with such passion and force. But she had: even to the point of angering one of her mother's pro-choice friends, who took her first opportunity to let Susan know. You too may be offended. Yet if you are to see Susan as a whole, you need to read this, the opening of Susan Austin's "The Aborting Community":

> Today a woman has not conceived a child until she has decided not to abort it.
>
> True, she may carry within her a mass of protoplasm with a unique chromosomal structure, exhibiting independent sensations, reactions, movement, and will; but there can be no question of this being a human being until, with godly power, she makes it so by her solitary word. To the relief, no doubt, of Justice Blackmun, who wrestled so vexingly with the question of when life begins, the answer has proved amazingly simple: When, like Darius lifting his golden sceptre to Esther, the gravid woman has signified her royal pleasure that the worthless intruder be not destroyed, at that very moment the mole, the tumor, the sticky mass of tissue becomes a radiant soul worthy of honor, medical care, and protection from nuclear power plants. But if she fails to lift the sceptre . . . her word of yea or nay is certainly

hers alone, and if not divine, at least divinely powerful. And because it is exactly her right to privacy that is deemed so deep, so all-conquering, so crucial to her humanity that it surrenders into her hand the power of life and death over her most helpless dependents, it is correct in a certain sense to call her fiat a private choice. Nevertheless it is absurd to say that she chooses privately. Behind her solitary will stands a community, the great Leviathan of which she is a member; and just as the result of her choice will filter through and influence the whole body, so the moods and reflections of the whole body will reach down and affect her choice. It is impossible that it should be otherwise: That she is in the position to make the choice at all is an affair of the whole community, including the Supreme Court. Furthermore, she has been reared by the community, has read its books and listened to its gossip; she knows what her friends think and what the woman's movement thinks; she has heard of doctors and seen children in the grocery store. We can be certain that she is not a Carthusian hermit, since unaided parthenogenesis is not characteristic of our species.

As an ethicist, I now judge Susan's most important point to be her analysis of the community's relationship to the individual: there are no individuals without communities. And so there can be private choices, but only because the community has allowed it to be so.

Susan also knew that it was important for people who believed as we did not only to try to persuade by words but also to live accordingly and to offer our own lives in service. She concluded "The Aborting Community" by pointing to hopeful signs of another community coming to be:

> Even now, in fact, there are arbiters of *boni mores* at work restraining people from this ruthless and bloody legal right. The nation has a conscience; there are bystanders who are appalled and ashamed, and they leaven the whole lump. The proof is that women who have abortions weep, suffer depression in cycles, form groups to suppress

their guilt feelings, have emotional traumas during subsequent childbirths, get angry with "society" for making abortion a harder experience than it need be, and write manifestos announcing that in a "society we can all live with" they (1) would not have to make hard decisions and (2) would feel no worse about abortion than about an operation to remove a mole. These women suffer from the condemnation of those who find abortion wrong; there are also women who are helped by the encouragement of those who find childbirth right: who speak up, volunteering to adopt; who help buttress the building, making suffering not only bearable, but transcendent. . . .

Amid this great cloud of witnesses is also the silent testimony of every person who finds it a good thing to be merciful to those in her power. Such private witness complements public action. To keep our conscience keen, to publicly condemn (and thereby restrain) this legal right, to turn the spirit of the community, Congress could enact and the President proclaim a national day of mourning for ten million children slain. On one day a year let us wear black armbands and announce for all to hear that killing babies does not advance the public good.

Children

Susan's passionate writing about children came from her heart. She always had wanted lots of children; she once mentioned that we should have eight. This was another wondrous and strange thing about Susan: I came from a small family with one brother; each of my parents had one sibling; I had no way to imagine a large family as anything other than utter chaos. But she was the third child of five (all sisters), and to have children, she knew, was the best thing she could do.

(There was also, to be honest, a bit of rebellion in it. Apparently her mother's sex education for her children consisted entirely of the need for population control. Susan remembered her giving out buttons to her daughters to wear: "STOP AT TWO," they said.

"But I'm number three," she told me with not a little existential exasperation.)

In preparation for our marriage we met with one of those rarefied countercultural birds that were among our friends in Santa Fe, a lay midwife who went by the name of Siva Moondance. (She had a baby whose name was Twilight Magic.) Siva taught us how, by monitoring changes in Susan's body temperature, we would be able to know when she was fertile and thus avoid having sex at those times. This now seems contradictory to Susan's desire to have lots of babies, but at the time it made sense. We were both thinking about seminary, and it seemed good to delay children. We didn't want to use chemicals on Susan's body, and the IUD we suspected of preventing the implantation of a fertilized egg, rather than being a true contraceptive.

After we were married, however, and thus after we commenced sexual relations, we realized that Susan's periods were too irregular for the temperature to be meaningful. We tried condoms and spermicide for a while, and then just gave it all up.

The truth is, we both wanted children, and it seemed to us that how children fit in with seminary studies was something we could simply work out when the time came. Another consideration was that we didn't know when the bishop would give his permission to go to seminary. It might be several years. (It turned out to be four.) Would it be good to wait so long?

Our first child might not have been a child at all. One evening Susan came to me with anguish. "Look in the toilet," she said. I looked and saw only a bowel movement. I flushed. She then told me she thought it was an early miscarriage. There had been no reason for us to think she was pregnant—no sickness, no body changes, and no "missed period" since hers were so irregular.

I often thought about that child, that mysterious might-have-been being. We don't know if it was a child, and because of my intemperate flushing there was no way to find out. It, whatever it was, was just gone.

These things move deep into one's unconscious. I recall an evening at seminary, sitting alone in the chapel in the darkness, praying to God for this possible being. And then decades later, just two or three years before she died, Susan gave me a little sheet of paper with names of people to pray for on All Saints' Day. She wasn't able to go to church that day, but I carried that paper in my pocket and the names in my heart. On that list was "Heather Felicity." Susan had given that potential child the name that, way back before we had children, I had proposed for a daughter.

Back to Santa Fe: Not much later Susan was verifiably pregnant. This child was conceived, it seems, on or near our first wedding anniversary, about a month after I started commuting to teach junior high math at the Santo Domingo Indian reservation. We had health insurance that, according to the latest regulations, covered maternity care "just like any other illness"—a description at which Susan rightly bristled. I remember our doctor telling us that his present partners were not as sporting as his former ones but that he used to offer a bet on the sex of the baby: double-or-nothing on the fee. His fee was about five hundred dollars, or about 5 percent of my salary as a teacher, so if it hadn't been covered by my insurance I would have considered the bet! (I think there is a house advantage, in that the heartbeat of unborn girls, I've been told, is on average a bit higher than that of boys.)

When Michael was born on July 4, after a day and a half of labor, I evinced unhappiness over the Caesarean section. But a wise friend said to me, "Victor, give thanks for modern medicine; mother and child are both alive." Yet Michael did arrive with a blood infection and so spent his first days in a pediatric intensive care unit. This meant Susan could not see him—she was kept in her room, and he in his incubator in another place. The next day we got Susan into a wheelchair and took her to see him. She leaned in and wrapped her left hand around his right arm. In the photograph of this first meeting, I see her wedding ring, her glasses, her unworried yet unsmiling face. His head is under a glass box for oxygen. He lies on his back with his knees splayed and an IV going into one of his tiny feet. There is a lot of technology in that picture (and yes, give thanks for modern medicine). And yet it is a picture of complete humanity, of normal and yet sacred love, the mother touching her child for the first time.

When you touch a child for the first time, the softness that you feel is the infinitely good gift that each of us is to each other.

Susan was discharged at five days, Michael at six, and we went about making a home for the three of us. Two years later I was approved to go to seminary, so we loaded up our earthly goods and drove to New York City. Susan continued to want more children, and we were doing nothing to prevent conception, yet no children came. We were trying to keep track of her irregular periods. I have a letter she wrote to me in July 1983 (i.e., before Emily). She was at her parents' home in Montezuma, New Mexico, while I was in pastoral training at a hospital in Albuquerque. In the middle of it is a short paragraph: "I have bad news about health—I am still bleeding and it seems to be getting stronger. Mark it in your little black book."

But later that year after we returned to seminary (and again it seems to have been on or around our anniversary), another child came to be. Susan found some midwives in New York City to see for her prenatal care, with the birth to come as we summered back in New Mexico. Emily was born on July 3, after a very short labor. Although by then sonograms had been invented (and we have a grainy picture, which was used to estimate the due date), we did not know her sex. The doctor had given Susan a "trial of labor," yet in the end Emily also was born by Caesarean section. I was in the operating room, and I remember the nurse filling in a form after the birth. She asked the doctor what she should put down as the reason for the operation. "How many do you want?" he replied. All I remember is that the first body part Emily presented to the world was her hand.

So we had two children for the last year of seminary. Susan had a job that year running a nursery for seminary students: an ideal job for her, actually, since she would get to be with Emily while taking care of other babies at the same time. She worked in conjunction with the seminary day care center, which was run by a friend of ours, Jack, a pacifist who would have fit in perfectly with Siva Moondance. Jack believed that children should learn correct names for body parts. One day he was explaining to the children that, before they were born, they were in their mother's "uterus." Another friend overhearing that said, "*Womb*, Jack; it's the *womb*." Then Susan weighed in: "I just say 'tummy.'"

(That same year I was a seminarian at Trinity Church Wall Street. One Sunday after services we were in the Trinity elevator with a number of well-dressed parishioners; Michael was riding on my shoulders. "My penis tickles," he said. In the ensuing moment of everyone pretending nothing had been said, my mind went straight to Jack.)

More Children

It was a couple of years after seminary. We were living in Wappingers Falls, New York, where I was the assistant priest at Zion Church. God had not given us any more children; we were finding sex to be pleasurably satisfying and were doing nothing to prevent children. They just didn't come.

Susan noticed an ad in the local paper. The county social services agency was looking for foster parents. She inquired and found that one could set limits on the children one could take; in particular, it would be possible for us to say that we'd only take babies. She persuaded me that this would be a good thing for us to do. I certainly agreed that it would be a good thing to do—and that Susan would find particular fulfillment in it. So we went to the training sessions and got ourselves and our home certified.

"This has been an exciting and busy year for us," she began our 1989 Christmas letter.

> *In February we completed the massive process of becoming certified as foster parents (we had started last October) and two days later we had our first foster child. Ramon came to us straight out of the hospital, 3 days old, so I quickly got back into the "up all night" routine. He was only 5 pounds, and I wore him in the Snugli everywhere I went, including all the services of Holy Week. Right after that, Social Services reclaimed him and he left us, by that time over seven pounds and with a lovely smile. I have since heard that he has been adopted and is still full of smiles.*
>
> *Our next foster child, Jonathan, came in May. He was five months old, and if Ramon was tiny, Jonathan was, and is, enormous. Jonathan was very difficult at first. He was a constant and inconsolable screamer, so we paced many a floor with him. But gradually that wore away, and he is now a generally cheerful boy with charm in buckets. He is still with us—we have seen him learn to sit up, crawl, acquire six teeth, stand, walk, and say "tree." He will probably go back to his family within a month, and then won't it be quiet around here! (That is, until Social Services gives us the next one!)*

Over about three years we had nine children altogether—only one at a time, and some for just a couple of weeks, but some, like Jonathan, for six or nine months or more. The social services agency particularly liked us because, since we were not looking to adopt, our interests were purely to care for these children for the time we had them without other complicating motives. Susan, being a stay-at-home mother, did most of the caregiving; that was her desire and her fulfillment. Here is how our son recalls it, in words he spoke at the interment of his mother's ashes in Santa Fe some twenty-five years later:

I remember one child in particular [not Jonathan] who would scream when he woke up or was hungry, and he wouldn't stop for anything, being picked up, anything. He had been born to a woman who didn't want others to know that she'd had a baby, so she'd leave him in the car while she was in work and he didn't know that crying made any difference. He was loved by Mama, and he learned to stop crying when he was picked up. Mama, like Mary, loved the sufferer, and always was a comfort to the afflicted.

There were also "crack babies," a girl with only part of an ear, a boy whose father had dislocated his shoulder, and so forth. They came to us while their mother or parents dealt with their addictions or other issues. We knew that none of these children would ever remember us. And we knew that often they would return to homes that still had big problems. But Susan would say that deep in their souls they would have a memory of being held, touched, cradled, cleaned, fed, and in general being loved. She believed that such a deep memory would not be lost and had the capacity to change a person's life for good.

I can't recall why our foster parenting came to an end around 1992. But it had concluded before the late spring of 1993, when Susan's tumor was found.

We had lots of pictures of these babies; along the way Susan collected one of each child and put it into a small photo album. When a couple of decades later our young friend (and aspiring actor) Andrew was helping her with exercise and trying to get her to talk more, he learned about these children and got her to find and show him the picture book. It's my sense that, in her years of increasing silence, when it was difficult for her to concentrate long enough to formulate her thoughts into spoken words, her soul often thought about these children. Quietly, of course, it was pro-life work and witness; she was one of those people she had written about in the *Human Life Review* who shows it is "a good thing to be merciful to those in her power." But pro-life witness is not why Susan got us into foster care. She got us into it because the babies needed us, and we could help.

The desire for more children never left Susan. During her chemo treatments and her initial use of antiepileptic drugs (which she needed after surgery until she died), we were afraid that these powerful medicines might harm an unborn child, so we abstained from sexual relations for a year or two. But then they resumed, as pleasant as ever. Susan was now past forty, and no child was conceived (that we know of). Yet I can remember, even just a couple of years before the end, the look in her eyes. "Let's have another baby," she said.

What did I say? I hope I smiled. But when I turned aside my head, my eyes were damp. How wonderful that she wanted children. How sad that her physical state was so out of sync with her mind.

2

The Middle

Lights

In the middle of the night, she was breathing heavily, strangely. "Susie, Susie," I called to her and tried to get her to awaken, but the noisy breathing continued. In my memory, its duration was half an hour; in reality, who knows? She didn't awaken. In the morning her tongue was bloody; she had bitten it in her sleep. We didn't know what had happened. It pains me to remember that I blamed her for not waking up.

A month later I was away for a couple of nights for a church meeting—what we called "Provincial Synod." I phoned her from Albany, as was our custom when I was away, just to say hi and find out how things were at home and to let her know I was okay. She said, "It happened again last night." What? "I woke up with a bloody tongue." But she said she was fine.

Earlier that year she had been driving Emily to a dance class. There was a car wreck behind her, and she suddenly felt horrible, although her own car was untouched. A brief diary entry first calls it a fainting spell but then says it wasn't fainting. "Did not know whether I would pass out or throw up. Hit like running into a brick wall. Lasted a few minutes. Afterwards completely normal."

I recall another event from that time. Again, Susan was driving our children after school. The signal lights turned yellow as she was going through an intersection. She suddenly felt very strange. She pulled to the side of the road and stopped the car, and shortly thereafter the feeling passed. She never lost control of the car, but she very much needed to get it off the road so that she could stop. She didn't know what that was.

But lights scared her after that.

(A year previous we had been driving on our vacation through Kentucky when a thunderstorm burst over us. There was lots of lightning and heavy rain. I was driving, but nonetheless she wanted to stop, to get off the road. This didn't make sense to me: Why should lightning so bother her? I told her we were quite safe from lightning in the car, and I insisted I could drive safely through the downpour. With obstinacy I pressed on. Now I wonder if there was, even then, something beginning to go wrong inside her, something I was too stubborn to notice.)

In early June the nighttime forced breathing and the bloody tongue happened again. This time we called our doctor's office. We belonged to a site-based HMO that was generous with advice over the telephone. But in this case the nurse instructed us to go to the emergency room, where one of their physician assistants would see us. The children were at school. I canceled whatever appointments I had and drove Susan to Poughkeepsie.

At the hospital, after the physician assistant had talked with us and checked out Susan's vital signs and run some blood tests (as I recall), he met with us again and said he really thought all this was caused by stress. Now I know that stress can cause significant physical symptoms, but we were much younger then, and that diagnosis struck us, frankly, as dismissive. Susan told him, again, that her father had died of a brain tumor. He grudgingly said, "I'm nearly certain that you don't have a tumor, but I know you won't be satisfied unless we check for it, so as a final test before you leave I'll order a CT scan of your brain." I left Susan there for the time it would take to do the test—by then it was midafternoon and I needed to pick up Michael and his cello at school and take him home. When I came back, maybe an hour and a half later, the PA met me in the hall. "I'm glad to catch you, Mr. Austin," he said. "I didn't expect this, but the CT scan . . . your wife does have a tumor."

I went in and sat beside Susan and held her hand.

How naive it now seems to me—how naive I was, not to recognize a seizure when it was occurring in my dear love beside me in bed; and how naive not to have connected the nocturnal seizures with her daytime "episodes" as related brain events. And how innocent of suffering, how oblivious to what was to come.

To Do What Needs to Be Done

"Brain tumor": two of the scariest words in the English language were now a fact of Susan's life and of mine and that of our family and our parish. At once I learned something important about myself—namely, that I cannot absorb Big News on first appearance. Perhaps out of sheer denial, but perhaps also out of an intuition that it had suddenly become my job to step up to new responsibilities, I refused to consider the things this might mean, for instance, that Susan might soon die and our children might have to grow up without their mother. Instead of entertaining any such Scary Thoughts, I suppressed them—it wasn't a deliberation, just an action. I put out of mind those fearsome prospects and focused on the immediate things that had to be done.

The first immediate thing fell within the hour. The children would need someone to take care of them once they were both home from school, to give them supper and so forth. I phoned Anne, a friend in the parish, who took the news on board with equanimity and faith. She offered to take Michael and Emily to her home, where they would spend the night while I stayed with Susan through her admission into the hospital, her first meetings with specialists, and her many tests.

This set the pattern for the rest of Susan's life, the next nineteen years. Whenever her health had a new downward turn—whenever a new chasm opened in front of us—I learned I could focus precisely on the concrete needs of the present. The question would be, "What do we do now?" Indeed, I often had the sense that God was with me, protecting me from being overwhelmed and strengthening me to do my best for Susan. I prayed at such times with simple yet intense immediacy, and I knew—I could *feel*—that God was giving me sufficient power and clarity to take care of the things at hand. Susan would recognize the title of this section as coming from Garrison Keillor's (imaginary) sponsor, Powdermilk Biscuits, which "give shy persons the strength to get up and do what needs to be done." God was often just that for me.

Yet it must be said that there is a dreadful cost. In attending to the needs that were at hand, I did not allow myself to look up and see what might be the bigger picture. The to-do list had my attention: Meet our HMO's neurologist. Get the medications that he has prescribed for Susan when she comes home from the hospital. Make appointment with a neurosurgeon. Meet him, check out his reputation, schedule surgery. Meet Susan's primary care physician, who is to coordinate all this. . . . When one of Susan's presurgical blood tests was ambiguous, we rushed into Poughkeepsie to get a new test done on a Saturday, but it was too late; the surgery had to be postponed. Reschedule surgery. . . . And so it went: the to-do list always had new things on it. There was always something to do *today* or *tomorrow* or *next* or *after we get the results*.

But never was there time given to wondering, What is the bigger picture here? Perhaps it would have been fruitless to wonder about it, since of course we did not know how things would turn out. I did, once, do a bit of pondering, when I laid this before my spiritual director. He said something that was, while not really saying anything at all, oddly helpful. There were three possible outcomes, he said. Susan might have her tumor removed and then return to ordinary health. Or she might die. Or she might survive but be limited in some way, not fully healthy. He advised me to pray about each possibility and then to accept whatever came.

This, I say, was oddly helpful, in that it gave me calm about everything being in God's hands and a sense that whichever way it turned out for Susan, God would be with her and me, our children and our parish. Nonetheless, as a day-to-day matter, the to-do list, with the many things that needed to be done, asserted its claim to attention.

Today as I am writing this I regret that I often focused on the immediate need to the exclusion of a longer, wider perspective. It is true that God, just like those imaginary Powdermilk Biscuits, stayed with me and strengthened me to do what needed to be done. But he did not open my mind to the unknown future. And I did not open my heart to the gut-wrenching thought that, having been given my heart's desire, a long process had begun wherein that gift was being taken away.

Prayer No Longer Makes Sense

Once Susan's tumor had been found in that early June, she was put on steroids to keep it from pressing too much on her brain until the surgery could be performed, which turned out to be nearly two months later. During those long weeks, the drugs made Susan puffy and tired. Her mother had flown out to help a little; she liked to take Susan for walks down and up our long drive. Her mother was good at walks and at most practical things, but she was a deeply worried person, particularly since her husband had died of brain cancer. Many years before, she had rejected all religion; she knew none of the comforts of prayer. Unlike, everyone thought, us.

It was one of our dry summers, and by early July the grass was only tiny sticks and dust. One afternoon Susan and I sat on the sofa watching our children play in the yard. They turned nine and thirteen that summer, and although we had withheld nothing from them, their child hearts could entertain no tragic thoughts. Mama had a brain tumor; she was going to have surgery; she would get better. We marveled at their love for play.

Across the yard from the rectory we could see the church. Everyone was praying for Susan and being helpful as only a parish can be, with daily offerings of food, car rides, cards, letters. So many cards and letters! Every day brought more, and every one of them brightly said, "We're praying for you." Some were humorous; some sentimental; many "religious." But always, behind the various flowers and pictures and icons, were a hundred attestations of prayer and spiritual support.

And as we watched our children, she said to me: None of this makes sense anymore. I feel my mother's concern; I see our children's love; I read all these cards. And I can't pray.

She who had introduced me to Mary, who had brought dozens of home rituals into our family, this very Susan was in the center of prayer—and yet prayer was for her as distant as the planet Pluto, as inaccessible as quantum physics. The inaccessibility of prayer was totally unexpected, like having a five-star gourmet dinner delivered to your door but finding (or feeling) that your nose no longer smelled and your tongue no longer tasted and, furthermore, your body no longer took in food.

Prayer no longer made sense. She felt simply but utterly disconnected. *I understand the externals. I see the exteriors. But I can't pray.*

What do you do when you can't pray? Do you just try harder, exert sheer willpower, and *make* yourself pray? I don't think so; at least for me, willpower doesn't get me very far by itself.

When Susan wrote about abortion, she saw that the individual and the community could not be separated one from another. The community shapes the individual, who in turn makes the community a little different than it was. Community and individual cannot get away from each other. In like manner, it seems to me, the prayers of a community can be strong enough to carry along an individual who is, at a given time, unable to pray. A sign of this is that in church each of us doesn't have to be paying attention at every moment throughout the entire liturgy. It seems to me that God arranges it so that at any given time at least one person is genuinely praying.

My bishop in those days, Richard Grein, once told us about an ordination service he had attended in Russia. His party was late in arriving (which, since the Orthodox services are so long, didn't matter a bit). As he entered he passed a man, vested, smoking a cigarette. "Are you serving in the liturgy?" the bishop asked. "No," he answered, "I'm getting ordained."

That could be an icon of Susan in those dry summer days: standing outside, aware of the incense and chant and beauty inside but unable to be *in there*. She was the focus of intense spiritual energy and yet felt utterly alien to it.

A couple of years later Susan was trying to explain what had happened to a friend who, in turn, was telling her that it's always possible to pray. I take Susan's side on this. Sometimes, I think, we just can't pray—and that's nothing to feel guilty about. In such times we may let ourselves be carried along by others; we can know that they are praying for us. We don't have to do it ourselves. To put it paradoxically: our own faith (in the sense of what's really true) can be a bigger thing than our own faith (in the sense of what we are able to believe and do at a given time).

Seizure Control

Susan's tumor was an astrocytoma, a star-shaped thing with tiny tentacles that insinuated themselves amongst her brain tissues. Her father had had a different kind of cancer altogether. His was the sort that could metastasize all over the body; Susan's would never do that. But it was impossible for the surgeon to remove it completely—to get all the tentacles would require the removal of brain tissue itself—so, when the postsurgery biopsy revealed it to have a midgrade malignancy, the experts took counsel with one another and recommended, given Susan's young age, that it should be treated aggressively, with both radiation and chemotherapy. The radiation was given daily, five days a week, for eight weeks—the maximum allowed. Then a brief rest, and the end of the taking of steroids, since there was no longer a need to keep down swelling (and our surprise that you can't just turn steroids off, that withdrawal is hard—no one warned us it would be). And then chemotherapy: a conjunction of three different drugs administered in six-week cycles. Susan was to undergo six to eight cycles; in the end she was doing chemo for a year.

The first and principal drug was a pill—actually, two pills, a double dose—taken at home. When it came time to take them, Susan and I just stared. There the capsules sat on our little saucer. They had cost us about eighty dollars (our insurance at the time covered half the cost of medications). We said we could go out and have a really nice dinner for the price of those pills. And we noted the irony that our dinner would probably not conclude with vomiting. Susan breathed her courage and swallowed. She was indeed nauseous later.

Her hair fell out. Her face remained swollen. Her body became a war zone of periodic chemical attacks. Every three weeks a clear chemo drug was put into her veins in the oncologist's office. (A decent man, he was later murdered in the parking lot of the Newark airport, reportedly for his refusal to turn over his wallet to some thugs.) On the fourth week of the six, she took a daily pill that gave her a rash. And then we came back to week one, and those knockout pills.

And then, after a bit more than a year, it was over. She had MRIs periodically: before the chemo, at its end, and every six months or a year thereafter. Her tumor never grew back. The doctors, expert life defenders applying to my wife the best medicine of the day, had indeed conquered her cancer. This was a success.

There seemed to be only one problem left after Susan's surgery, and that was to keep her seizures under control. Seizures were expected, not as being caused anymore by the tumor (for it had been removed) but as a result of the surgery itself. Susan's post-surgery seizures were not convulsive, but despite her medications she experienced what seemed to be partial seizures. As I came to understand it, a seizure would start somewhere in her brain but not go through it all, and it would then stop. I could be immediately beside Susan when one of these was happening and not detect anything. But Susan knew they were happening. She would need to sit down. Then she'd go to bed, and she'd be exhausted for a day.

Her neurologist said that seizures cause seizures, so if we could just find the right medicine, then her seizures would get further and further apart, and eventually she could be seizure-free. This became my goal and my preoccupation over the next half-dozen years—focusing on the to-do list, on what needs to be done, and not on the larger picture. But although Susan tried a variety of anticonvulsant medicines, she didn't go more than a month without one of those seizures. Nothing seemed to work.

Meanwhile, underneath this and unsuspected by us, a disease was working its way within her brain. About 1999 we changed neurologists, and Susan got renewed and careful attention. That's when we heard for the first time the words "white-matter disease." It may have been on account of this white-matter disease that, on the Christmas I have described, Susan just went to bed. Her brain, although cancer-free, had been injured by the radiation (most likely) and by the chemo and the surgery (to a lesser extent). It just wasn't able to hold things together as well as it should. And it was gradually getting worse.

The truth, it seems, is that her seizures were indeed being largely controlled by the medicines she took (and it didn't seem to matter very much which medicines they were; they were all along doing their work). For most of her days there would be no seizure; on occasion, a partial seizure would break through. But having such a seizure once a month, or (over time) even just once every other month, or (as was the case a decade later) even just once a year— that was not such a bad situation. That was not something worth worrying about.

For the first five years after her cancer treatments, I had been focused on one thing (seizure control), which caused me always to be looking to the future, to be hoping for a day when Susan wouldn't need those medicines and would be back to a seizure-free, normal life. But in reality, she was in better shape at that time than she would ever again be. In reality, her brain was slowly, slowly, slowly deteriorating.

Where Was God?

Where were you, Lord, while this was happening? The Susan you had given to me was slipping away, and you didn't tell me. If I had known, I would have done different things. I would have cherished those days just as they were, rather than striving for better days.

He Taketh Away

Our human relationship with God is a dynamic of giving and receiving, bestowal and counter-bestowal. This is the way it is within God's own being. The Father loves the Son, which means he bestows himself upon the Son. The Son receives this gift and also gives it back to the Father. And the gift that is between and around them is the Holy Spirit. There is nothing to God except these relationships. God is entirely love, and love is entirely dynamic: given and received and given back.

It is so beautiful, this description of the Trinity. And I would stake my life on it. Indeed I have, and I will.

But what happened to me is that this dynamic came close to home. Too close.

Love was given: Susan came to me as my wife.

Love was received: We lived together for fifteen years and had children and foster babies and many other joys of love.

Love was taken away: Susan had a brain tumor, and its (yes, successful) treatment began a disease in her brain that started taking her away from me.

It took nearly twenty years. But God is persistent. As the psalmist has it: "like a moth you eat away all that is dear to us" (39:12). He took Susan away from me.

On the Other Hand

Think about the Eucharist. The people come together and offer themselves to God. The symbol of that self-offering is the bread and wine that is placed on the altar. In the early church, each person would have brought some bread and wine, and it would all have been gathered together, some of it being placed on the altar, the rest being set aside to minister to the poor. (Wine, of course, was ordinary drink, and it would all have been local wine—so my liturgics professor, Thomas Talley, reassured us—and thus could be commingled into a common vessel without fear of it foaming or turning green.)

That bread and wine on the altar is then transformed, by means of the eucharistic prayer, into the Body and Blood of Christ. And then that sacramental bread and wine is given back to the people.

In short, in the Eucharist we give ourselves to God, and God accepts our gift and makes it better, and then gives our selves back to us. In this exchange of gifts given, received, and returned, we become once again the Body of Christ.

This is a much more positive way of understanding the dynamics of love. It begins with us, and it ends with us, and we don't die in the process. Yet in that eucharistic prayer there is death: the "remembrance," which is the making efficaciously present of the self-sacrifice of Jesus, his own death on the cross. Right: we go to church; we make our offering, which symbolizes our self-offering; we receive the sacrament, which is our own offering transformed into Christ; and we go our way rejoicing. But in the midst of it is death, and the only reason the Eucharist "works," the only reason, that is to say, that we have the joy of our life, is because of that death in the middle.

When Jesus the Son of God receives the Father's gift, he freely gives it back. The gift is his own being, but it is also his relationship with the Father. He cannot be himself apart from that relationship. To be himself, Jesus gives himself fully. And in the world of human beings in which we actually live, to give yourself is to die.

God Intends to Kill Us

Fast-forward to New York City, sometime around 2010. I have invited the young adult fellowship to our apartment. Susan has gone to bed (at this time she is sleeping ten hours or more each night). About twenty people are sitting on chairs or on my floor, and one of them is going on in a sentimentally pious way about how God loves us and if we just pray and trust him everything will be good. This person is taking up a lot more airtime than is fair, and I get annoyed. "I don't think that's true," I say.

All eyes turn to me.

"And," I continue, "I don't think that's what the Gospel says."

Doesn't it say we should trust God and he will take care of us?

"No," I say. "At least as I read it, the Gospel says that God intends to kill us. And in the end he will succeed."

As they come out of my mouth, those words surprise even me. But here's what I was getting at. Every one of us is going to die. There are no known exceptions (except for Enoch and Elijah and, possibly, Moses). Jesus healed a lot of people—but later they died. Jesus even raised Lazarus from the dead—but later on Lazarus had to die again. If it weren't God's will for us to die, life wouldn't be as it is.

You can't get away from this. You could say, the only reason there's death in the world is because we sin, that death is a consequence of sin. Okay, I say, but God is responsible for there being a world in which death is a consequence of sin. If God didn't want it that way, it wouldn't be that way.

Or you could say, in any imaginable physical world there are going to be chance events, and one of those chance events is death. That is, you might try to argue that any material world at all will have to have death as part of it. Okay, I say, but even if that were true (and I'm not sure it is), it would not take God off the hook. God, after all, did not have to make any material world at all.

Does God indeed take aim at us, or did I stretch the point when I said he "intends" to kill us? God certainly does not become another created agent of death, one option among many, as if a person might die of cancer, or of a heart attack, or of murder, or of God. So he cannot intend to kill us the way a violent intruder might. On the other hand, the psalmist speaks of God shooting arrows at him: "your arrows have already pierced me" (38:2). It is our tendency to turn away quickly from this relentlessly hard side of God, rushing over to more comfortable considerations. But Psalm 37 ("he shall give you your heart's desire") is followed by Psalm 38 (the piercing arrows) and the desperately low Psalm 39 (which ends asking God to go away, so that the psalmist might die in peace).

It is God's intention that we die. And since he is God, he will surely succeed.

The Executive Function

Susan had many friends through our church, and they kept visiting her and doing things with her. Some of these friends worked out exercises for her and would "work out" with her with some light weights at home. Others would take her for walks. They did better for Susan than they were aware, because, left to herself, she would have done nothing except read books.

Her book reading used to fuel her creative activities, such as her arts and crafts, inventive home rituals, cooking, and writing. I have mentioned only a sampling of these. In her active years, every day seemed to bring a new development with a children's story, or a new picture in one of several media, or a new ritual for our family involving festive foods and music, storytelling, and much more. These things Susan would have discovered by herself through her reading. She would read a craft book, say, and then create something that was inspired by it. But now, posttumor, postradiation, postchemotherapy, taking daily antiepileptic drugs, her preference was to sit and read, or to go to bed and read. She was retreating to an inner, and inactive, world.

A couple of times over the years of her brain disease, she saw a neuropsychologist. The first doctor met with her alone, with us together, and with me. He helped me have insight into our situation. One thing he helped me see was how remarkable it was that Susan had no depression. However much she may have been aware of her deterioration, she did not seem to be "down." (In fact, a remarkable quality she had to the end was her ability to smile at people and seemingly if wordlessly connect with people of all sorts.) I can recall only one instance of "down-ness." It was in the late 1990s. Susan is sitting at the dining table while I am in the kitchen; it's in the evening. She looks to me and says, "I haven't always been like this, have I?"

The neuropsychologist explained to me that Susan's "executive function" was compromised. This was likely a result of the location of Susan's tumor, and in any event it was clinically evident to him. He taught me that it is our executive function that keeps us on task. I may be writing this book, say, when I notice across the room something that interests me. My executive function tells me to keep writing for now and check out that interesting thing later.

Susan lacked this executive function. Consequently she couldn't do things like plan her day. She wouldn't see that she needed exercise in order to keep her health. She couldn't persist in any task if she saw something else that she wanted to do.

And what did Susan want to do more than anything in the world? She wanted to read.

She loved to read her favorite books: Jane Austen, Charles Dickens, Tolkien, the Narnia books, Agatha Christie, Georgette Heyer, Josephine Tey, and lots of children's books, including, as they were published, the Harry Potter stories. She could read these endlessly. She could loop back to the beginning just as soon as she reached the end. Generally, she preferred to read books she already knew.

If Susan saw a book that interested her, she would stop speaking even in midsentence, forget whatever it was she was doing (or whoever it was she was talking to), and start walking over to the book.

The neurologist said to me: *You have to be her executive function.* "It's hard," he said. "You don't want to be giving directions to your wife. But if you don't, no one will, and she can't do it on her own."

This was the bind I was in for at least ten years of our marriage. In many ways, I had to treat my wife, my life partner, the mother of my children, God's gift to me of my heart's desire—I had to treat her as if she were herself a child.

How That Worked Out

I made daily lists for Susan, and she hated them. She would complain about them to doctors or friends. But they did help her. At one point, say, the list might have read:

- wash dishes
- go outside and walk down and up our hill
- write a thank-you card to Anne
- lunch: PB sandwich and some of the leftover salad
- nap: don't take a book to bed
- I'll be home about 4:00

I knew there was a problem with the "nap" item, because by saying "don't" it might actually put that idea into Susan's head. But the reality was, she would take a book to bed whenever she could and then spend the entire afternoon in bed, not napping only but napping and reading and not getting up. This was bad for her physically and was also an occasion for her to close in on herself even more. So the message was to use the bed for sleeping and to sit in a chair for reading.

She was particularly stubborn about this, and I struggled over it to the very end. Indeed, after she died, I found some books that I had removed from her when she was reading them in bed.

It was awful, and I often felt I was doing a terrible job. I was bossing her around, then getting angry with her when she dis-obeyed. I would try, calmly, to explain why the lists were good for her, and why the various items on the list were good for her; she'd say she understood, and we'd hug each other, and I'd cry. And the next day it could be the same all over again.

I'd wonder: what a strange situation this is! I have a wife who wants to smuggle Charles Dickens to bed, and I'm getting angry over it! Susan never watched television (we just didn't have TV, never wanted it). She would, in her final years, have been happy to watch videos of her favorite movies (like *Casablanca*, *Mary Poppins*, *The Trumpet of the Swan*). Yet the movies she wanted to see, like the books she wanted to read, were all wholesome, comforting classics.

I had to say no to her, even though I was saying no to something that was not at all bad in itself.

In addition to this existential bind—having to be the executive function for my wife and thus having to be a parent to her—I was also in, to use a fancy term, an epistemic bind. I never knew for sure what was the case with her condition.

If Susan was sleeping a lot, I did not know whether (a) she was sleeping too much and needed to be roused and encouraged into some physical activity, or (b) her body was needing that extra sleep because of its frailty and woundedness. There is such a thing as sleep causing sleep, and with her brain injury, she might not be able to get herself out of bed when it was time to do so. "Sleep is nice; let's just sleep some more." I was sometimes afraid that she would hasten her death by just sleeping away.

But I never knew for sure. It might have been that she needed sleep and that by getting her out of bed I would be harming her.

I erred on the side of pushing, but it was dreadful; I never had any confidence about how much I should push or encourage her and how much I should step back and just let her be.

I've talked to a lot of people who have to care for others whom they love, and we always recognize this point of commonality. One woman told me that her husband, who had a particularly virulent cancer, was panicking and crying out. She made the reasonable assumption that his panic was caused by withdrawal from some potent painkillers, which he had recently stopped taking. She tried to comfort him and told him everything was all right. A few days later she learned that his lungs had been filling with blood and that he was quite rightly afraid that he was drowning. How could she have known?

The "epistemic bind": having to act with and for another person without knowing what action (or inaction) would be truly helpful. I say I erred on the side of pushing. When Susan was in her last year, an old friend told me that she used to think I was really hard on Susan. She had known us for more than twenty years. We were having coffee at Le Pain Quotidien; Susan was in a nursing home rehab center at the time. Our friend said, "But now, Victor,

I think you were very good for her. I don't think she would have lived this long if you hadn't been so firm."

It is comforting to have a friend tell you that you've done well. Yet inside it hurts. It still hurts. I never wanted to be her boss. I hated having to take over her executive function.

Evil: Take One

When God made the world, it was good. There was light and dark, day and night, sun and moon and stars all working together harmoniously. There were plants and fish and birds and creeping things and beasts of the field—all living in one beautiful ecology. They grew and flourished and enjoyed the plenteous wonders that were everywhere around them. Fish and bird and creeping thing and beast of the field did not feed upon each other; they ate plants instead.

Then God made his most special being of all. This being was given the exceptional gift of freedom. A choice would be put before him: whether to take in all the goodness of the world and say yes to God, a yes that would be manifested by his free acceptance of his place in creation; or, such being the awesome gift given by God, to say no and choose a path of disobedience that he would tell himself was a path of self-creation. Instead of accepting his place, he could strike out to make his own place.

It was not necessary that this creature choose disobedience. We can imagine that, faced with the choice of whether to obey God, he might have freely chosen obedience and thereby acquired a knowledge of good and evil that would be qualitatively different from anything we can imagine. For in such a case this creature, ever expanding in love and glory, would have rejoiced in all things and freely been creative as only he could have been.

But the creature chose otherwise. And at once, all creation fell from its happy state. Animals and other creatures started feeding upon one another. Man and woman were alienated from the once-good created world, and from each other, and from God. In the very next generation, fratricide would enter the world. And not long after, there would be the multiplication of every imaginable human sin.

Still, it is better for there to be this kind of world that we know than for us to be unfree. Evil is in the world because God made us free, free to love or not. God could not have made us free without risking that this is how things would turn out.

Evil: Take Two

About fourteen billion years ago, the entire universe was a singularity, a point. It was immensely dense. It had no past (whatever past there might have been would have been erased in that compacted singularity). The universe then exploded, and within tiny fractions of a second fundamental laws of physics were established. According to these laws, the simplest atoms came to be and, over a few billion years, compacted into stars. In the center of these stars, more complicated atoms were made, one of which was carbon. Another five billion years or so, and the universe had a lot of different elements in it. Around this time our sun was formed, and, orbiting around it, our planet.

In the primal soup of the Earth, from time to time, a cosmic ray would fall in a randomly significant way. Gradually, living beings of increasing organizational complexity emerged from the soup. These beings were challenged to survive and to reproduce. Those that were successful, succeeded. That's a truism, but it is a centrally important truism. Some other types of beings did not survive. But evolution needs the eruptions of chance, those occasional cosmic rays that mix things up. And it needs chance from other sources as well. Sometimes a mutation, an alteration, turns out to be advantageous to survival. And so it goes.

We human beings would not be here today apart from the long-established laws of physics underlying the processes of evolution, which require the interplay of chance and necessity.

Now when a person gets cancer, it is one of those chance things happening. If it were impossible for cells occasionally to mutate, we humans would never have evolved into existence. We would not be here if cancer were not a possibility.

The very same laws—the interplay of chance and necessity—that underlie our existence also undermine our existence.

This is another way of saying that physical evil is in the world just because it is a world. The earth has to have a molten core; thus there will be earthquakes and volcanos and tsunamis. Lions must eat, and so lambs will get eaten. Wind must blow, and so grand rock formations will collapse. Everything is transitory. Everything decays.

Evil is a necessary correlate to there being a world at all.

Evil: Take Three

We must continually remind ourselves how strange God is.

For God to create something means for God to give it existence. Creation is not the same thing as anything we humans do. I might make a chair, but in doing so I use materials and tools that are already at hand. I might compose a symphony, but in doing so I use things like pitches and instruments and pen and paper (or computer!), things that are already existing. When God creates, he simply *gives* existence; he doesn't use things already at hand.

Or, if I make a chair, the end of my making is the beginning of the chair's existing as a chair. When I was only half done making it, it wasn't yet a chair and thus wasn't something to which you would want to entrust your posterior. And if I am composing a symphony, the symphony doesn't exist until I'm finished; only then can it be performed and come to real existence as an experienced work of music. If you tried to play a half-finished symphony, it might not be music at all. You might end up pulling your hair out, or racing out the door screaming.

But when God creates, he does not begin something or launch it into existence; rather, he *gives* it existence. Creation, properly speaking, is the same thing as "holding in being." If it were possible that something had no beginning—if, say, the universe were temporally infinite at least as regards going backwards in time—then God, if he created this possible thing, would just be giving it existence as it is. Aquinas, interestingly, seems to have thought that the idea of a universe with infinite past time was a coherent idea and thus something that God could have created. (He thought that the universe had a beginning, not because he thought that any created thing must have had a beginning, but because he interpreted the Bible as revealing that the universe had a beginning.)

So to create is not to make, and it's not the same thing as starting or launching or beginning. That's strange enough, one might think, but there's more.

Everything that exists is good, and it's good precisely insofar as it exists. This is true of beings, and it is also true of things that beings do.

So if you have a cat, God is the creator of that cat, which means God gives that cat existence, God holds your cat in being, and your cat is thereby good. And if your cat scratches its ear, that act of scratching is something that God is the "cause" of—he causes that action just as much as he causes the cat to exist by sustaining it in being. And so that scratching of its ear is good also.

Obviously, if we were smart enough we could explain why the cat scratches its ear in terms of biology and physics (and perhaps psychology, depending on your view of cats). Nonetheless, it is also the case that God causes that action, because it is something the cat does and God causes everything that is.

What we don't want to say is that "after" creating the world, God "stepped back" from the world and let it start running on its own. It is true that the world runs according to laws, and it is true that God gives those laws to the universe, since he, as we are saying, gives the universe its existence and continues to hold it in being. But the point about creation, as the giving of existence, is that it is something God just does. It's not something God *did*. God never "steps back" from the creation.

To think that God steps back is, in fact, to indulge in a bit of idolatry. It is to think of God as a really big, really powerful *thing in the world* who has to step back or else we wouldn't have any space for our own action.

But God is much stranger than any idol. Your parents might need to step back from you in order for you to have freedom. Washington may need to step back from all of us in order for us to have freedom. But God, who is no idol and who is no thing in the universe, has no place to step back into. He can't "distance" himself from the universe because "distance" is an idea that makes sense only within the universe. God is not an idol; God is not in the universe.

At the same time, freedom is manifestly real. If I do something freely—say, push your cat aside so that I have a place to sit on your sofa—that is an action that is a real action only because God "causes" it. In other words, it is a real action because God gives it being, even as he holds me in being while I do it and as he holds your cat in being while it hisses back at me.

This is Aquinas's view, and as I understand it, it contradicts portions of what I wrote in "Evil: Take One." It is to say: *God causes my free actions.*

But Aquinas also seems to hold the views of "Evil: Take Two." That is to say, he holds that a material universe will contain *evil suffered*, the sad consequence of there being a world at all. (He, of course, had no idea of the age of the universe or of the laws of chance and necessity.) Yet he also holds that there is *evil done*, which occurs when free beings freely choose to diminish themselves by choosing a lesser good rather than a greater one. Such actions are not really actions at all, and thus God does not cause them. If I take a really nasty turn and shoot your lovely cat, God still would hold me in being while I did that, and he would hold your cat in being until I was finished. But he would not be responsible for my choice of shooting your cat rather than loving it. That is the strangeness of "evil done."

Now we come to the mind-blowing, confidence-shattering, vertiginously terrifying conclusion. "Evil done" does no good. When a lion eats a lamb, the lion flourishes, but when I needlessly do in your cat, I just diminish myself, make myself less human. There is no point to sin, no point at all. Which means that since "evil done" does no good, *God could have created a world in which it would have been impossible.* God could have created a world in which there was no evil done.

Why didn't he?

God does not answer. We might not be able to understand the answer if he did. We cannot escape it: God remains exceedingly strange.

The Hip

It was Holy Wednesday in 2001, and Susan was getting up slowly from bed. I got impatient. "I have to be at church for Morning Prayer," I told her, "and I'm going on over. You'll have to come by yourself and you'll be late."

(There I was, laying it on that she had to live by the consequences of her actions, without any moderating tenderness to acknowledge that things like getting up were hard for her.)

We lived, as I've said, across the drive from the church. A couple of other people were there for Morning Prayer, and we started, and Susan did come in later. Afterwards, one of them (Susan's friend Theresa) walked home with her while I stayed in the office.

When they got to our door, Susan turned to marvel at the daf-
fodils that were bright in the sun, and she fell. Theresa felt awful
that she didn't have Susan's arm, but who could have foreseen the
fall? I myself had earlier left Susan to walk to church by herself.

I came over, and we helped Susan to her feet. Susan and I went
inside, while Theresa went home. Susan's leg was hurting, but I
thought (as usual) that she just needed to push through the pain.
She couldn't sit, so I got her to lie down on one of the children's
beds. I had a class to teach at Marist College that morning. I
checked on Susan a bit later, and her leg was still hurting.

So I called her doctor's office and reluctantly canceled my class.
With difficulty I got Susan into the car. At the doctor's office, she
couldn't walk; we asked for a wheelchair. Inside the office, she was
in pain and unable to remove her pants. The doctor said that they
couldn't help her there; they wouldn't even be able to position
her to take an X-ray. An ambulance was called to take her to the
hospital. I drove and met Susan there.

Her hip was broken: the femur, up close to the ball that goes
into the hip socket.

I had been making her walk on a broken leg!

The orthopedic surgeon said that, since Susan was young, they
would try to pin the bone rather than doing a replacement. After
pinning, the bone might grow back together. This doctor didn't
know Susan's history, although he knew she was on anticonvulsants, and so they would need to take precautions for the surgery.
I failed to communicate to him that she was, in effect, much older
than bare chronology indicated and that it was hard for her to
remember and follow instructions. For instance, after this pinning surgery she would have to avoid putting weight on that leg
for months so that the bone might heal. Were those instructions
that Susan would be able to carry out? It didn't seem likely, but I
didn't raise that objection clearly. The doctor too was young, and
my thoughts were narrowed onto the immediate picture, and so
they went into surgery.

By now it was nighttime; the surgery was over about midnight. I had paced the floor of the hospital and had begged God to give me Susan back.

My Church Friends

John, an old priest friend who worked in the bishop's office, left me a voice message when he learned of Susan's broken leg. He said that I would have every reason to ask God, "Why me? Why this?" It was a comforting call. He assured me of the bishop's concern.

Susan came out of surgery okay. But she started doing weird things. A day or two later she stopped eating. She wouldn't talk to us. I tried to play with her food to get her to eat. She'd open her mouth as if to receive the forkful of food that I held, poised in midair, but as I brought it to her mouth she would clamp shut, keeping the food outside on the fork. She'd smile, wordlessly.

Did they give her too much medicine during the surgery—too much of the anticonvulsants? Or was it the anesthesia? Or (I now wonder) was it a sign of her brain's ongoing deterioration?

I did the evening services of Holy Week without Susan. Given her great love for them, it was extraordinarily odd for her to be absent. Michael was away at college in California. Only Emily was at home with me and able to share the liturgies. Our parish had a truly great Easter Vigil—our favorite service of the year, and one that Susan loved especially. It began at 11:00 p.m., in darkness, and had in the middle a great burst of light and the ringing of bells that people brought from home, and a lot of joyous alleluias. And then about 1:30 a.m. we repaired to the undercroft for a huge potluck breakfast and buffet. There were many children underfoot—and some in sleeping bags. But this year there was no Susan.

On the afternoon of Easter Day, I was back in her hospital room. She now was on a rehab floor but needed help in eating, in everything. Bishop Sisk came and prayed for her and comforted me. I didn't expect to see him; it was a great gift.

(He later told me that, looking at Susan, he didn't expect her to live. Nearly twelve years later, at her funeral, I reminded him of his good visit.)

Susan took three weeks to recover. She got physical, occupational, and speech therapy in St. Francis Hospital. The therapists there got to know her well, and she made amazing progress. She went home and received more therapy there. Yet her hip did not heal. Four months later, she had to have another surgery, this time for hip replacement. Then, again, after surgery she was "out of it" for three days. This was immensely frustrating—why couldn't it have been prevented? I wondered what I might have told the anesthesiologist that could possibly have made things turn out differently. (Now I suspect that her brain just couldn't handle anesthesia.) The therapists, remembering her from April and understanding her needs (and, yes, loving her), persuaded the insurance company to keep her in the hospital for rehab. And again, in three weeks, she was able to be discharged.

That was early September 2001. She had outpatient therapy for a couple of months and almost got to where she could walk without assistance. But she depended on a cane for the rest of her life.

Hydrocephalus

In the months that followed Susan's hip replacement, she developed other problems, including what we learned to call, rather delicately, "urge incontinence." This led us to yet another specialist, a nephrologist, a doctor who specializes in kidney function. This new doctor performed her examinations of Susan and ordered various tests but was able to come up with no answers. None of her tests found anything awry. But since one of the tests was an MRI, and since I had always brought Susan's other MRI films to her neurologist, I did so also with these—notwithstanding the "reading" by the staff radiologist that they were unchanged from Susan's previous MRIs.

As the neurologist studied the films, he was thinking also about Susan's more recent problems and her fall and broken hip the previous year, and he was led to a preliminary diagnosis of hydro-cephalus. It made sense: pressure from excess fluid on the brain could cause the brain to malfunction in various ways. He consulted a neurosurgical colleague, who agreed. "Hydrocephalus": a new term entering the lexicon of Susan's ailments.

Thus it happened that a year after her hip replacement, and almost nine years after her initial brain surgery, the healing arts were again applied to her skull and its contents. To treat her hy-drocephalus, a hole was drilled through her skull, and through that hole a tube was inserted to the center of her brain. The other end of the tube was spliced into a vein in her neck. There was a pro-grammable valve on this shunt: it would open, and her brain fluid would drain, only if the pressure in her head were above the setting on the valve. And that setting could be adjusted—programmed—externally at any time in a doctor's office. To adjust the valve, a magnetic device would be placed on the side of Susan's head.

Susan's programmable shunt became, in the years to follow, one more thing for me to keep in mind and bring to each new doc-tor's attention. For instance, because of her shunt, Susan could no longer simply have an MRI, since the magnetic field created by an MRI is strong, potentially messing with the valve setting on her shunt. So after each MRI, Susan's brain shunt had to be reprogrammed. It fell to me to make sure this happened and to know the correct setting for the valve.

The changeability of the setting, however, may have worked to Susan's benefit at times. When we moved to New York, the oversight of the shunt fell to a remarkably humane pediatric neu-rosurgeon (Howard Weiner—his walls are covered with pictures of and letters from children he has helped). He periodically reviewed her shunt's condition and gradually reduced the setting over a few years. We thought we could perceive some improvements in Susan's functioning.

But the immediate consequence of Susan's brain shunt was that she was not allowed to fly for the first several months. We had not been told beforehand about this restriction. It meant that Susan was not allowed to go to California to attend Michael's college graduation. Theresa came and stayed with Susan for that long weekend, while Emily and I flew to the ceremony. I will admit to mixed emotions about this. There was regret that Susan could not be with us. Yet, in honesty, it felt like time off. I was free to visit with many of Michael's college tutors (as they called their professors) and to go to many events, which, had I been caring for Susan, I would not have enjoyed.

Graduations

In 2002 we had altogether four graduations: besides Michael's finishing his BA, I finished my PhD at Fordham, and Emily finished high school. And Susan was not to be left out. Our parish awarded Susan her own graduation certificate. It read:

The Wardens and ad hoc Social Committee of the Church of
the Resurrection attest that
SUSAN L. AUSTIN
has successfully (and calmly) dealt with three operations,
two school plays, one senior prom, the birth of a doctoral
thesis, and in the midst of all this has successfully completed
enough physical therapy to be classified as
AMBULATORY!

We had a picnic on the lawn in June and invited the parish. Susan smiled, the center of a party swirling around her.

Prevenient Grace

It is profoundly paradoxical and yet true that the internet, a cultural artifact that strips us of so many things that are personal, nonetheless fosters social relationships. In its own day the telephone did something similar, connecting by voice people who, on account of distance, were unable to touch each other. (Advertising, of course, ever tries to appropriate the negative features into a positive metaphor. If you are of a certain age, you may recall the advertising slogan to encourage the use of long-distance telephoning: "Reach out and touch someone." The thing distance made impossible—touching—became a metaphor for speaking.)

My friendship with Nick, the fellow who moved to Santa Fe with me after I graduated from St. John's, went back to high school. We could spend hours talking every evening without tire. He was a Catholic and, while at college, had considered becoming a Dominican priest. Even after we had gone to our different colleges, when we came back to our hometown on holiday we would meet, go to an all-night truck-stop restaurant, and sit for three hours drinking coffee, talking about the Bible and sacraments and the priesthood and whether celibacy was a good thing; we'd also talk about politics and the Christian concern for the poor. His wit was never dormant. When we paid the check, Nick would add a large tip. "For the parking meter," he said.

But just four months after persuading my friend to move out to Santa Fe with me, I had moved out on him. For years, I remembered this as a fault on my part. I had abandoned my friend, who lacked a car of his own, and left him to live in a couple of rooms in a house far from the center of town. After marriage, I saw him only rarely. Four years later I left town to go to seminary. And that was the last I saw of him.

I had heard that he had married a young woman he met in the acting program at the College of Santa Fe and that they had moved to Colorado. Occasionally I heard a tiny bit of news about him or his old Oklahoma family. But there had been no contact for decades, not since Santa Fe.

So it came into my mind one evening a few years ago that I might, as we have learned to say, "google" his name. It came up—on a program for the production of a small theater company in Colorado. I wrote to the company a brief explanation of who I was and asked if they would forward my email to this person who had the same name as my friend from many years ago. In a few days I had a brief note from him and then some longer letters. Finally Susan and I were able to visit him and his wife at their home near Denver. It had been thirty years since our marriage. We had together a long, pleasant day of learning what had happened to each other over the past three decades.

This story is, it seems to me, although a good word for the internet, also a story about God, the unseen character who works in the background of things. Theologians speak of "prevenient grace." By that term we mean God has a way of giving us grace before we ask for it. Sometimes God goes ahead of us into a situation and prepares things. And he had done just that for me.

For years I had the sense that I had done badly by my old friend, that I had caused him to move five hundred miles and then abandoned him in a strange town while I went on with my happy life. I felt guilty about that. And I was thinking, as our meeting that October got closer, that one thing I wanted to do was to ask his forgiveness.

But here's what happened: When we met, when late into the day I started describing this as I have written it here for you, he started laughing and interrupted me and corrected me. "Vic, it wasn't like that at all," he said. He knew before he moved to Santa Fe (something I had forgotten completely) that even though she had rebuffed me, I still wanted to marry Susan. He had felt no abandonment; rather, he had begun a new chapter of a rich life that he looked back upon with humor and delight.

I don't think this is peculiar to me, although it certainly is true of me. In this instance with my old friend, as in many instances over the decades of taking care of Susan, I looked back on things I had done and had a regretful feeling that I had fallen short, that I hadn't done as good a job as I could have. At times, I still have these feelings. I don't feel an utter failure, of course; I can also see that I've done some good. But it's never simply black or white; it's always in between. Mixed in with the good there is always a lot of me falling short.

Yet, wrapping around all the ambivalence of my care for Susan, there is the unseen character of this book, the one who sends grace ahead of me. How good it is, now, to hear the voice of my old friend, my friend who was best man at our wedding and still, even as I write this, cares for me. "Vic," he says, "it wasn't like that at all." And he laughs.

We Never Doubted God's Reality

I state this just as a matter of fact. It is an aspect of God's surrounding grace for us. We didn't labor to have faith in God; we didn't consider the evidence and come to a conclusion; it was just the case. Throughout our life together, from our first days of walking to church in Santa Fe to the end, neither Susan nor I ever doubted that God is real; that his Son, Jesus, took on a human nature and lived fully a human life; that Jesus died on the cross and rose to new life on Sunday; and so on—the basic tenets of Christian faith. We never considered that God might have been a convenient illusion, or a childhood fable, or some other sort of immature comfort that we should now grow out of, particularly given the cancer and its aftermath of progressive debilitation of Susan's brain.

We always knew God was real and Jesus was real and that he, Jesus, had been a dead man and was now alive.

Yet the grace of faith did not shield us from darkness. As I've written, during the summer when her brain tumor was found and operated on, Susan found it impossible to pray. We knew God was real then, and we also knew there were other people who were praying, but in the center of her being, there was no experience of prayer at all. She couldn't do it; she couldn't understand it.

The benevolence of God has often been dark. I have known God is real, but his love for me, it seems, has been an awful love. "Smile, God loves you" was never a bumper sticker on my car. "God loves you; run for your life" would be closer to my thoughts. Dear T. S. Eliot says we will "Die of the absolute paternal care" of God that always goes in front of us—"prevents us," in the old language—and will not leave us alone. It is telling that the poet puts the verb at the emphatic first place of a new line. If we do well, we will . . . *die*, die of God's care. Oh yes, God is real all right.

Back to College

I had discerned an unfulfilled aspect of my vocation—namely, to teach. We were much loved at our parish church. I had been there many years, including the years of my doctoral studies in theology, and the people trusted me as their priest in countless ways. But it seemed to me, and to those friends to whom I turned for counsel, that I should venture forth and seek a college teaching post. And if I were ever to do so, I needed to make the move while my doctorate was fresh. So in the year following my receipt of the PhD, I applied widely to a number of colleges and universities. Mount Aloysius College, a Catholic institution sponsored by the Religious Sisters of Mercy, offered me a position in the faculty of theology, philosophy, and religious studies.

To move out to this college in western Pennsylvania would be disruptive. I would leave the church pension system and could expect my pension to be frozen at its current level. I would leave our comfortable faith community, where we had raised our children and where I had been the spiritual leader for most of my adult life. We would leave a network of friendship and support for Susan. We would leave her doctors.

Susan, I remember, was opposed to the move. She told me I had promised the parish I would never leave them. This cannot have been true—no priest ever makes that promise, nor is it a promise that is even possible to make. That she said this to me was a sign of her condition, at the least. It may also have reflected fears that she couldn't otherwise articulate.

So I had to work through many things, and it was agonizing. Could I leave the comfort and security of the parish? Yes. Could I accept and could we survive on the salary cut that I would be receiving? I worked the numbers, and the answer was yes. Would my retirement be jeopardized by the move? Again, the numbers indicated things would be okay. Would Susan be able to have good medical care? Here the answer was only a qualified yes. There seemed to be good doctors in the nearby city of Altoona, but for anything serious, she would have to go to Pittsburgh. The reputation of Pittsburgh's medical facilities is very high, but they would be a hundred miles away.

Would it be good for Susan? It was at least possible that there would be benefits for her. A new situation would challenge her mind to learn new things. This might be good. New doctors could have new insights; this also might be good. We were going to live in a second-floor apartment in a complex with some open grass and surrounded by trees. So, while alone during the days, she could get the exercise of walking our steps and enjoying the grounds. On the other hand, she would be alone for many hours, five days a week, as I taught at the college, which was to be a half-hour drive away. I—we—would have to trust God that she would be able to handle herself. This was scary.

I took my fears to my friend Hillary, a priest and psychologist who had accompanied me over several years with prayer and spiritual counsel. We met in the food court of a shopping mall for several hours as he helped me face these fears and trust God and do what, yes, I felt he was calling me, and Susan with me, to do.

Thus in the end I chose—and it was I who had to make the decision, not us, as once again I felt the awful and heavy consequences of her deficiencies in the executive function. Our children, both now at the University of Dallas, were supportive, although of course they wouldn't be at hand for day-to-day help. We packed up, said our good-byes, and moved in August 2003.

To be honest, I took the position at Mount Aloysius simply because they would have me. The college was remote, lacking much high academic life. But I knew that the best way to get a teaching job is to have a teaching job, and I thought that, after being there for a few years, I might get called to a better college.

But something surprising happened. I came to love my students. Many of them were the first in their families to attend college. Some were older learners, for instance, women who had children and had been previously discouraged from developing their minds. They were eager, if unskilled. I developed a special capstone class that emphasized citizenship, and we worked from a number of primary texts, such as Plato's *Apology*. I got them to read a bit of Hugo Grotius, the seventeenth-century Dutch theologian (and philosopher and lawyer), on punishment. And we read a *relectio* on just war by the Spanish Dominican theologian of the sixteenth century, Francisco de Vitoria.

These texts worked. Just as the founders of the Great Books program at St. John's would have said, great books were written for everyone to read. What higher gift could there be than to give my students that direct encounter with good books!

So by the summer of 2004, I was feeling this might be the college where I would teach for the rest of my life. I was planning some changes that would make it better for Susan. One of the sisters—we knew her as Sister Ginny (she has since died)—told me I should figure out how to bring Susan to school. We could find a room for her to sleep in during the day, when she wanted to; she would enjoy the library; and there were lots of students who could get to know her and maybe work with her. I liked Ginny's enthusiasm, and indeed I think it could have worked out.

But one evening there was a voice message on my cell phone. A very timid voice identified himself as Andy Mead, rector of Saint Thomas Church in New York City. With many hesitations, he asked if I would have any interest in coming to his church and being a theologian on staff there.

Back to Church

Our move to New York City in January 2005 brought many medical opportunities for Susan. She became a patient of a neurologist who brought order and simplicity to her anticonvulsants; she eventually was taking Keppra only, although at a high dose. And there were several years when she had at most one partial seizure, or even none at all. Many other studies were done, but their benefit was only negative—they ruled out other possible hidden problems.

We moved into a clergy apartment in the Saint Thomas Choir School, which is in Manhattan, about half a mile from the church itself. The rector's wife, Nancy, took a shine to Susan and often would walk with her to church on Sunday mornings. Susan's strength improved. She also received physical therapy from time to time, which trained her in gait and balance. For the next four or five years, Susan's physical condition did not decline, and in some ways she improved. She still needed to nap. She still needed a lot of sleep. There was no increase in her executive function. But surrounding those stubborn facts was a new environment that, I now judge, extended her life.

Living in the choir school, Susan was able to share in the meals with the community there. This community includes some thirty boys ranging in age from eight to fourteen, their teachers, and other staff, including housekeepers. The headmaster told me that her sharing in their meals was not only a gift from the school to Susan but was also a gift that the school received from Susan. The boys would have, as it were, an encounter with an important reality whenever they had Susan in their midst. Here was a woman who walked slowly with a cane, who was hunched over, who loved to smile, and who was hard to communicate with. It was good for them to see her and to see that she was loved and valued too, not for what she could do, but just for who she was.

With Susan, I too joined in their meals at times, but she could also go alone. This was thus a gift also to me, in that I didn't have to worry about Susan having good and nutritious meals. (The Saint Thomas choir boys eat food that's as good as any on the planet, honest.) By this time Susan was not able to do any unsupervised cooking. When she ate with the boys, I was free to be working elsewhere and not to have to return and check on her. This made midday meetings and evening classes at church possible for me.

Also by this time—more than a decade after her initial brain surgery—Susan was unable to take care of her own medications. They had to be laid out carefully each morning and marked, lest she take too much of one and none of another. For this reason alone, someone needed to be with her every night. In addition, she got almost irrationally anxious if I were away.

So in order for me to attend the occasional academic conference, Emily made arrangements to return home for several three- or four-day periods each year. Susan liked having Emily around— while I was away, they would eat lots of pancakes and grilled cheese sandwiches, and Emily would read to her old children's stories like *Winnie the Pooh* and *Make Way for Ducklings*. And they'd watch the films of Humphrey Bogart or cartoons like *The Trumpet of the Swan*. The two of them thus shared a return to childhood, albeit with the roles partially reversed.

Susan Walking

It was good for Susan to be at the choir school, and it was equally good for her to be in New York City. She always said she hated the city—it was a near-complete opposite of the New Mexican mountainside on which she grew up—but in fact she liked the bustle of it.

If you've never lived in New York, it can be hard to imagine: life is possible without owning a car. My Oklahoma relatives asked me, "How can you live without a car? How do you go shopping?"

My cheerful answer: "We walk! New Yorkers do a lot of walking."

Susan had real difficulty in walking, particularly since that broken hip during Holy Week. With me on the sidewalks of New York, she would walk more slowly than most people, her cane clutched in her right hand while her left clasped onto my elbow. The city's sidewalks can be crowded. There are treacherous unevennesses in the surface; there are pushy people who seem oblivious to the danger they pose to frail walkers. Susan never went out alone, but once we got outside, she found the world fascinating.

She would see things that I don't see when I'm walking alone—alas, I'm usually one of those pushy walkers. She looked with delight at the variety of folks all around. She saw the gnarled trees and the black squirrels of Central Park. She saw babies, and dogs, and joggers, and sports teams. She loved to stare at a parade going by, or a woman with a colorful umbrella, or a group of children skipping and singing. She also saw the homeless.

We would turn the corner from our apartment onto Seventh Avenue, and there, sitting on a plastic crate by the never-used pay phone, would be a man rattling a cup asking passersby for change. He said the same thing to everyone—except to Susan. "How are you, little lady?" he asked, and she would stop to turn her face to him. She was smiling.

There was a saxophone player on Fifty-Seventh Street; she wanted to give him some money. (She always wanted to give money to musicians.) Down around Fifty-Fifth Street she smiled at the man sitting in a wheelchair; he paused his normal chatter to greet her.

It's not that they knew each other, these panhandlers and homeless people and my wife. It's that they recognized something in each other, something they had in common.

Once we were walking home from the Museum of Modern Art, bundled for the cold. As we finished crossing the street, Susan tripped on the curb. Even now, it is for me the stuff of nightmare, played out in slow motion. Her body starts to fall; her hand slips a bit in my arm; she twists; the cane clanks on the concrete; I hear her head make its thunk. This time she landed on her back, and indeed it was a slow fall. I thanked God she was conscious—I remembered earlier falls, and concussions, and the broken hip.

"Little sister, are you all right? Are you all right?" The voice came from a man sitting at the corner by the building. He had a cup in his hand, a cup he was still shaking. You could hear the coins clinking against each other, but he had stopped his repetitious asking for change. Instead he was saying, was repeating over and over, "Are you all right?"

She was. I helped her up, and she brushed her coat down, took her cane from me, took my arm, and turned to him. "Yes, I'm all right," she said.

Those Earlier Falls

There were two falls back in Hopewell Junction. One Saturday Susan and I had gone out to lunch—to a place we enjoyed in the nearby town of Fishkill—and then we had gone to the Bass shoe outlet. Afterwards we were walking to the car. I was impatient that Susan was walking so slowly. (This was before she broke her hip in that fall during Holy Week in 2001.) I went ahead of her to get to the car, thinking, perhaps, that I'd stash our shopping purchases in the car and then go back for Susan, when I heard the thunk.

I turned around. She was facedown on the concrete, her eyeglasses broken, blood on her face. She also wasn't talking.

"Help!" I cried, but there was no one there to help. We were on a back side, it seemed; I ran around a corner, futilely trying to get attention. It took a long time. Finally someone came; finally an ambulance was called; finally Susan was taken to Vassar Hospital in Poughkeepsie.

By then she had her consciousness back—in fact, it was back before the ambulance came. It seems she had suffered a concussion. X-rays and CT scans showed no injuries. The ER had been slow, even for an ER; we had been there for at least eight hours. But they discharged Susan, cautioning me to keep a close watch on her for the next few days. She didn't go to church the next morning.

A few months later, on a Friday evening, I was coming back from a day retreat and had just turned into the long, gently winding drive up to our church and home. I saw, at the far top of the hill, Emily and Susan taking a walk down the drive. They stepped to the side, and I watched with frozen terror as Susan tumbled backwards beside the road. Emily lamented that she hadn't had her hand, but this was still a year or two before the broken hip of 2001.

I drove up beside them. There was no bleeding this time, no broken glasses (Susan had hit her head on the back). But again she was unconscious.

A driver saw us and came up the hill, asking if we needed help. We thanked him but said no, she would be all right. We were, I think, embarrassed, even though that didn't make any sense.

Susan came to in a few minutes, and we walked inside. It was Friday, so according to custom I ordered a pizza. Half an hour later we were sitting around the table eating it, when I finally decided I really did need to phone the doctor's office about this. When the doctor on call phoned back and learned what had happened, she recommended going to the ER. I asked if I could drive Susan there. She said okay, if I wanted to take the risk.

Well, that settled the question of whether to go in, although I did drive. Again a long wait; again various X-rays and scans; again no problems noted. After uncountable hours, the ER doctor came and, just like the last time, apologized for the long time we had been in the ER and said we could go home, but cautioned us to be alert, especially over the next few days.

I remember those two falls and those concussions, the unconscious minutes; I remember that fall on the street of New York; and I remember her last fall, the last fall of her life, the one that can still haunt my memory and make me cry.

3

The End

The Return of the Seizure

New York, Thursday, July 7, 2011, sometime between six and seven in the morning: I'm still in bed, awake but not yet up, and Susan is sleeping beside me. Suddenly she starts breathing heavily, noisily. Her hand clutches tight, she's on her side, and she curls, her knees jerk up. "Susie, Susie!" I cry, and I try just gently to hold and stroke her head, her hand. It stops. I know what it has been.

Now calm, she is sleeping. I take inventory: no bleeding of tongue. She has wet the bed. Other things seem fine.

This has not happened since—since when? Since before her surgery. Since 1993. Ever since then her medications have controlled her seizures so that, while on them, she has not had a tonic-clonic or grand mal seizure. But here she just had one. What does it mean? Why?

I think about those questions with part of my mind; with another part I move to take care of Susan. In a half hour she is awake and has no recollection of what happened. When I tell her, she doesn't seem terribly upset, although she is tired and doesn't like that. I help her to the shower, and I change the sheets and get the laundry going. I help her get dressed and have breakfast. We sit and talk a bit. At nine o'clock I get through to her neurologist, who calls me back and says she should have an MRI and a seventy-two-hour EEG (one where she gets the wires glued to her head and then comes home and carries around a recording pouch for three days). The rest of the morning is involved in making those appointments. Susan feels okay but tired. She is perhaps rather glad that I'm going to let her sleep for much of the day.

Each of these exams is a hassle: getting to the hospital or office is no simple thing with Susan. After the MRI we have to get her shunt reprogrammed before we can go home, and for that we have to wait for a neurosurgical intern to be available (for instance, to come out of surgery), and even then the intern doesn't exude confident knowledge of what to do with Susan's shunt (it is, I learn, an earlier model). So that single seizure has turned into a lot of things to do over the following week, which I have to work around my other work at church. As I've learned, it's possible to do this by focusing on what has to be done.

Eventually all the results came back: negative. What was it? We don't know. The neurologist thinks it prudent to raise the dose of Keppra. Otherwise, we go on with our lives.

And Another

In October we took a week's vacation in Phoenix, where our son and his family were living. Lucy, our granddaughter, loved to have Grandma visit, particularly since she liked to play with her cane. During our visit there were incidents of Susan strangely overheating—it is still hot in Phoenix in October, but even so Susan seemed to shut down too easily. She simply stopped being able to move her feet and walk. We tried to get her to drink water often. Still, despite those overheating occasions, the vacation included a lot of joy.

On the last day we had an early flight, nonstop from Phoenix to Newark, leaving before seven o'clock. I was awake in our hotel room at three o'clock, awaiting the alarm that was set to go off shortly, and then I would get Susan up and get to the airport. Suddenly: heavy, noisy breathing. Convulsions. Jerking.

It was happening again. "Dear Lord," I prayed, "help us! Help me!"

After five minutes—I watched the clock—the seizures stopped. I had no idea if we would be able to get to the airport on time, or if she could fly at all, but I wanted intensely to be back home, fearing being stuck thousands of miles away from Susan's doctors. So, not allowing the least thought about what it all might mean, I focused once again on what was right in front of me: doing what had to be done. I took my own very quick shower and dressed and was praying constantly for help, for the clarity to know what was the right thing and for sufficient strength to do it. About twenty minutes after the seizure had stopped, Susan was awake but visibly uncomfortable, and she couldn't control one side of her body—one hand could squeeze mine but the other couldn't—and she was unable to talk. Fifteen minutes later she was able to stand (if I held her) and talk. I got a washcloth and gave her a sponge bath. I got her dressed. She was weak and didn't remember the seizure, but wanted to help and was able to smile. I just threw her urine-soaked nightclothes in the trash.

Somehow I got the car loaded and helped her to it. When we got to the car rental return, just as I was worrying about how far we'd have to walk, a bus pulled up directly in front of us. The driver helped us on. When he left us at the terminal, a man was there at the sliding airport doors. He saw us and came towards us. "Do you need a wheelchair?" he asked. We eased through security with his help. At the gate, Susan wanted to go to the bathroom. We looked for a family bathroom, but there was none in that terminal. So she took her cane and entered the ladies' room alone. I stood outside with her wheelchair. Five minutes passed, then ten, then more. A couple of women noticed me. "Can we help? Are you waiting for someone in the restroom?" They went in and found Susan and helped her out. She was wearing her customary smile: Andrew, who had worked with her a lot that year with exercise and singing and talking, used to say that when Susan smiled anyone would do anything for her.

She told me she had had a large bowel movement, and that she was okay. This, if true, was a relief—there had been no movement for five or six days. But she was also drooling, and the saliva was orange colored. This was a mystery I never solved; it was as if she had been nauseous a bit, yet she wasn't coughing or gagging.

We went to the gate. I had Susan in the wheelchair and asked the agent if we could go ahead and board. She moved us to the front, bulkhead seats. Her supervisor beside her said, "Give them A and C, and leave B empty." We had the whole row to ourselves, and even better, the restroom on the plane was directly in front of us.

We looked out the window and watched Phoenix recede in the harsh early sun. It was awesome in every way I could think. At each step, someone had been there to help us. We were now on the plane. We would get home without incident. It was a miracle.

About half an hour into the flight, we looked out at a mountain covered with snow. Susan said to me, "It's been ages since I was on an airplane." I said, we were on a plane just last week, flying to Phoenix. Do you remember? She said she didn't. Her seizure apparently had erased that memory.

When I think of God being with me over all the years I was with Susan in her illness, it is this morning that I particularly remember. He gave me strength and focus to do what was necessary to get Susan ready. He protected her walking to the car. He got the bus there for us and then the wheelchair. He guided us through security. He sent those women to help Susan in the bathroom. He moved the gate agents to give us seats by the restroom on the plane. God was always with me, and he was with me in love.

That love of God is not in every case an easy thing to receive, but this is one day that I receive without hesitation or cavil. Despite his awfulness, the third character in this story is indeed a good God. And if ever I doubt it, I just think back to October 11, 2011.

This Time in Hospital

The next morning, back in our New York apartment, we awoke as normal. Susan had gone to the bathroom by herself at five o'clock and returned to bed successfully without accident. I got up at six, telling her I would work for a bit but that she could sleep another hour. At seven, she took her shower unassisted, as normal. She said she wasn't feeling perfect but was okay. She got out of the shower and dressed herself as normal (I heard the toilet flush during this time). But then her dressing was confused; when I went into the bedroom about eight o'clock, she had started putting on her bra but didn't yet have on her panties and her incontinence pad. I returned to the bedroom about twenty minutes later and found her lying on her back in bed, fully dressed, with the covers partially over her. She had a blank stare. The right side of her face was drawn down, her mouth asymmetrical. I asked her if she knew me, and she shook her head (but didn't speak) "no." When I asked her to squeeze my finger: her left hand could squeeze; her right hand could not. Since she had had accidents with her previous seizures, I asked if she was wet. She nodded yes. With her weak right side she wouldn't be able to walk to the bathroom. So I got a towel. She understood what I was doing and, with knees bent and both heels flat, lifted her bottom enough for me to slide a towel under it. It was now a quarter to nine.

These were signs of a seizure having occurred, but I had heard no sounds from her. So whatever the event was, I did not witness it.

By nine o'clock she could talk and squeeze with both hands. I had just written out a description of these morning events, and I left her to go downstairs to use the school's fax machine to send a note to her neurologist. When I returned, she was again vacantly staring. I got her neurologist on the phone and found that her left hand, now, was unable to squeeze my finger. Had she had yet another seizure?

Her neurologist said to go to the New York University hospital, where someone from his group would be expecting Susan.

The ambulance EMT, on the drive there, was getting information about Susan from me. She didn't look so bad. When I told him that Susan's doctor had said to go to the hospital, he rubbed his thumb back and forth across his fingertips. "Probably he needs money for a fancy new car," he said. I felt awful. I was trying to do the best by Susan, and here was a cynical health-care provider messing with my mind.

Emergency rooms in New York City seem to be crowded always, and this morning was no different. Before any neurologist arrived, the ER doctor ordered a CT scan. Needless, the neurologist intern later told me; what Susan needed was an MRI. That was eventually taken, and it showed no problems. Susan's shunt was reset, although with difficulty; they took an X-ray afterwards to confirm the actual setting of the shunt. (It was 110, as desired.)

Susan was in the hospital for three days. She had wires attached to her head for a continuous EEG, with a video camera turned on her so that, if she had a seizure, they would have both the EEG data and a visual record. But no seizures were seen, not even so-called subclinical seizures overnight.

Susan's neurologist decided that he had to blame the seizures on Ritalin, which Susan had been taking at a low dose since January to help her brain work a bit faster. Although the doctor thought it highly unlikely that Ritalin could have caused her seizures (either in July or now in October), there was nothing else to point to. Her anticonvulsant medication was increased to a higher level, and she was discharged. We took a cab home. She was tired but returning to normal. Her accidents weren't repeated. Obviously, no one knew what was going on.

Why I Witness to These Details

There is an appropriate human reticence to speaking about such things as incontinence. I would not, during her life, have spoken publicly about these things in such detail as I am giving my readers. Here, however, it is important not to keep every such thing behind a curtain of modesty. For these are in fact ordinary human things. They are common to many people.

If you, reader, have ever had to help your dearly beloved to the toilet or had to wash soiled sheets, you know what I mean. Everyone reading this book—indeed, every human being—needs to know that when such a thing happens, we are not alone.

On September 29, 1978, I vowed to love Susan as my wife in sickness and in health for as long as we were both alive. The events that I am recounting are nothing but parts of that reality, a very human reality. Our bodies, which can give us such pleasure, are also the loci of basic material needs. And sometimes, perhaps more often than we think, we need others' help with those basic needs.

But I want to say something more. It is *not only* that I had to do these things for Susan, things that I did not foresee and for which I was usually quite unprepared. It is, also, *not only* that in doing these things I found God to be with me and, in the tensest moments, to be present and helping me through. It is this: *I found joy* in doing these things. Wiping Susan's bottom, when I had to; washing sheets; guiding her through the obstacles of an airport; taking her to the hospital; sitting by her bedside; shuttling from home to hospital to work and back again; being her advocate in the midst of the frustratingly complex medical system and being the only person who knew her history and the many pieces of her complex medical case—doing all these things for Susan and upon and beside and for the sake of her body *gave me a joy I did not expect*. I would weep. I would be angry. I would pace the floor. *But there was joy in my bones*. I learned things about myself that I would never have learned. I learned that I could clean Susan's body and feel joy.

And this is not just the joy that's about me, joy that *I, the (ahem) great Victor Austin*, could do such a thing. And this is not just the joy that's about her, joy that *she, the beloved Susan Austin*, felt relief from the touch of the washcloth. It is a joy that wraps around both of us and lifts us up, in the midst of such a mundane human thing as caring for one another's corporeality—lifts us up to the heights, to the heart of joy.

Jesus, we are told, wept the night before he died and sought another way. His body must have jerked uncontrollably when the nails pierced into nerves. But as he looked out upon his fellow humans, might there not have been at that very same time, and without subtracting from the reality of the pain, might there not have been an elevation, a lifting up, a sense of joy?

"The love of my eyes has turned ugly," one might say. She lies unconscious. Her clothing smells. When I ask if she knows me, she just stares. But she is still lovely. I can stroke her forehead. I can kiss her lips.

I discover that joy is at hand, accessible, even in this.

The Pebble Dare

To take up a Lenten discipline, Father Mead once said, is to put a little stone in your shoe, a pebble that reminds you that you are walking toward the cross. Our lives are not aimless stretches of eating and working and spending and sleeping. We are going somewhere. Lent shows us that the Christian life is a pilgrimage, an ongoing road on which we follow Jesus and carry our cross, which is also his cross.

The pebble in the shoe is a metaphor not only for particular Lenten disciplines—the money we give away or the food we abstain from eating or the prayers we say—although it includes all that. The pebble in the shoe is a poetic way to talk about carrying the cross of Jesus. It's only going to be in our shoe if at some point we picked up that cross. And having picked up Jesus' cross, the point will come in our life when we lay it down. Life thus has the shape of Lent: at the beginning we put the pebble in our shoe, and at the end we take it out.

But it only starts—the Christian life only starts—if at some point we grasp the beauty of Jesus. If he were not in some way (and truly) beautiful, we would never have gone after him, never have fallen in love with him. He was of course beautiful as a baby, and beautiful as a young man; but he was also strangely beautiful when he was bloodied and abused and did not strike back. There was beauty when he talked with crazy people; beauty when he touched dirty and sick people; beauty even in his rare angers. None of us has seen Jesus in the flesh, and yet this beauty of his is in our grasp. And once we know his beauty, there's no way we could ever forget him.

When I was a teenager, I was fond of the music of *Godspell*, and in particular a very simple song, "By My Side." But it was only after Susan's death that I grasped something that perhaps should have been obvious: that when the singer speaks of a pebble in that song, she is referring to the cross of Jesus. This singer has grasped Jesus' beauty and wants him to take her with him. We listeners can fill in what he says—if you want to follow me, you have to take up your cross and walk—but the song has only her words. She says she'll put a pebble in her shoe, and then she urges him to watch her walking. Like a child in delight, she proclaims, "I can walk!" Speaking, as I believe, of taking up the cross, she says she will "call the pebble dare." She says they can "talk together about walking," which may mean that Jesus can explain the meaning of discipleship, but of course it is wonderful just in itself, without any further purpose, to be walking with one's beloved. Yet an end will come, and at that time, she says, she will take the pebble out of her shoe and tell it, "Meet your new road." And there at her end, she sings of taking Jesus' hand, glad, at the finality of her life, that he is, as the title says, by her side.

Such a lovely song for the big picture of our life, whose beginning is figured indeed in the Song of Songs: "May he smother me with kisses" (1:2). We fall in love with Jesus, and then we walk our pilgrimage, and when we "have had enough," at the end of the day, at the last night, we throw away the dare that we carried, the pebble—we let others, in their ongoing pilgrimage, carry the cross—as, at the moment of our death, we squeeze Jesus' hand, and he takes us, cross and pebble left behind, from the darkness of the grave to the light of the banquet.

Now this has happened neither to the person writing these words nor to you who read them. For us, at this point, it is only a picture, and Lent is merely a season. But those others whom we've known, others whom we loved, others who loved Jesus, others who have reached the end of the road of their pilgrimage and shaken off the cross: as they let go of our hand, did they grab hold of Jesus'? Is that, I wonder, how it happened with Susan? And I wonder: When it comes for me, the moment when I pass on the pebble and all it represents to those who continue their earthly lives, when I enter into the darkness of my own tomb, will the song then be true? Will I take Jesus' hand? Will I be, indeed, finally glad?

The Year That Would Be the Last

The Year of Our Lord 2012 began, and I went to the annual conference of the Society of Christian Ethics. Although I had been a member for a number of years, this would be the first conference at which there would be a discussion around a book that I had written. It was, thus, an academic and intellectual milestone for me; I looked forward to enjoying it. I took the train to Washington, D.C., and checked into the hotel. This was Thursday; the conference would begin the next morning.

But in the evening I got a call from Emily, who, as she had so often before, was staying with her mother while I was away. Her news: at supper, Susan had begun to jerk her body. One leg was straightened and stiff. Emily didn't know what to do.

Susan was still responsive to instructions but was not speaking. I phoned her neurologist's office; the doctor who called me back said we could wait overnight and see if Susan was okay the next morning, or we could take her to the hospital. Emily thought she could help her to bed and get her to swallow her Keppra. I remained in Washington.

Susan may have been in some sort of seizure state all night long. In the morning, Emily couldn't get her out of bed. She was not convulsing but was stiff. She wouldn't respond to speech. She certainly wouldn't open her mouth to swallow a pill.

So from Washington I called the doctor, who said, yes, emergency room. "Try to get the ambulance to take her to NYU, where we can take care of her, but don't be surprised if they just take her to the hospital that's closest." Which, to Susan's likely harm, they did.

A confession: there was a part of me that was really mad about this—mad, irrationally, at Susan. I would not get to stay at the conference and have the discussion around my book. Yet there was no question about what I should do, and indeed what I really wanted to do: get back home as soon as I could. The hotel let me check out without penalty; I told the conference secretary the brief story so that she could cancel my book discussion; Amtrak let me pay them about four times my original fare to return home early. I was at the hospital by early afternoon.

The doctors had by then come to the principal diagnosis for Susan of hyponatremia—namely, a low sodium level. They had Susan in intensive care for a couple of days while they gave her sodium through a needle in her neck. Her body temperature got really low, and for a while she was wrapped in a thermal blanket. Then they found she had a fever and diagnosed her as having an unidentified infection. So they started her on a powerful antibiotic.

Many elements of the hospital scene depressed Emily and me. I was never introduced to one doctor who was overseeing Susan's care. Instead, there were many doctors—this being a teaching hospital—but it was not explained to me how they would rotate on and off the ICU. For example, on the first afternoon there was a particular doctor who comforted me with the news that she had obtained the cell phone number of Susan's neurologist (at NYU), but the next day, this doctor was not around! Had she passed on that cell phone number? Had she been able to communicate with Susan's neurologist? What had they said? No one knew! I despaired of their communicating effectively with her neurologist or with me. The next day Emily overheard someone she presumed was a head doctor berating and insulting the interns in public, in the central area. The patient they were talking about was Susan. It did not inspire a sense of quality care. The focus was on low sodium and on the infection that they thought Susan had—and not on her neurological state.

In a couple of days, Susan had awakened. She recognized me. She was visibly uncomfortable, trying to scratch herself and re-move wires and other sorts of medical paraphernalia, and hence her arms were restrained. This was horrible to watch. But when I went to look for someone to talk to, no one was available. Nurses or clerks at desks would say they would tell the doctor, and time would pass, but no doctor would come. How was one to get the attention of appropriate medical people? In fact, it was only on Tuesday, Susan's fifth day there, that I first had a doctor truly listen to me. An intern, he would not let my concerns go unheard and unaddressed. He promised he would change her antibiotic and give me copies of her CT scan and her bloodwork. He also said that he would help us arrange transfer to NYU. Suddenly people were interested in us, and the paperwork was completed in short order, the insurance approvals obtained, a bed secured for Susan at NYU, and in the early evening Emily went with Susan in the ambulance across town.

In those days, according to my well-honed practice of nearly nineteen years, I found myself excluding from my consciousness everything that I could keep out of it. I didn't meditate on what all this meant, nor did I linger with remorse. I prayed intensely for discernment and wisdom, to make the best decisions for Susan. I focused on *what needed to be done*. I did what I had to at church. I said my masses and left Susan with Emily that Tuesday evening in order to go teach the opening session of the rector's doctrine class (he was on his Christmas vacation). My calendar even indicates that I went to the gym every couple of days. But for many hours each day I was with Susan and trying to understand what was happening with her, trying to get her back to the physical and mental place where she had been.

At the Epilepsy Unit

After teaching that class, I went to the epilepsy unit of the NYU hospital, where in the late evening I found Susan in a cool and quiet room. The neurologist on duty talked with me for a long time as I told her the story of Susan's illness, from the brain tumor to the most recent seizures. She then ordered continuous EEG monitoring of Susan—the same as she had had in October, when she was there for three days. The nurse suggested I spend the night in case, if Susan became agitated, I might be able to comfort her. She didn't have to make that suggestion twice. A bed was made for me beside Susan's, and I slept fitfully. Susan slept through the night. At eight in the morning some students came in. Her own neurologist came at about nine thirty and ordered various tests and also a visit from an infection doctor. I had comfort again that Susan was in hands that understood her.

It took several days, but Susan gradually returned to normal consciousness. I have a photo of her in the hospital bed, a feeding tube going into her nose, an IV into her arm, her glasses on her head, and in her hands *The Cricket in Times Square*. Her attention is focused.

Her body, however, did not quickly respond. She didn't seem to be able to swallow, and there was concern that she would aspirate her food and risk pneumonia. She had had a feeding tube that entered through her nose since her second or third day in the hospital. But a nasal feeding tube is not good for the long run. So, with the fear that she couldn't swallow properly, a "PEG" was put into her stomach. This is a surgically implanted tube through which nutrition and medicine can be given.

How good it is to have friends! Emily had many—she was in Opus Dei by this time—and almost every day someone from "the Work" would come to visit Susan. Sometimes there would be a group of young women surrounding Susan's bed, singing hymns and Christmas carols and old folk songs. Their voices and harmonizations were beautiful—although, I think, any singing at all sounds awesome in a hospital room. Another regular visitor was Andrew, the young man who had helped Susan the previous year with exercise.

During this hospital stay Susan had some physical therapy, brief sessions where the therapist came to her. She wasn't able to do much. At first it was just getting into a chair to sit for a while. By the very end, she started to walk a bit and was able, with help, to get from bed to bathroom. It was a major accomplishment for her, with assistance and constant coaching from the therapist right beside her, to walk the length of the hall. In fact, in her final days the nurses found her progress so remarkable that they urged that she be reevaluated for inpatient rehabilitation therapy. Alas, the evaluating physician remained unimpressed. He did not think she could handle its challenges.

This is a catch-22 situation for someone like Susan. A decade earlier, after her hip surgeries, the hospital nurses had to fight to keep Susan in the inpatient rehab unit. They were successful, and their judgment was proved right in that, as Susan returned to normal, she was able to make significant progress. The catch: she needed that intensive help to begin making progress. But here at the NYU Rusk Institute, Susan now being a decade older and the evaluating doctor not knowing her history, the gatekeepers were not willing to expend those resources to help someone who was not already giving evidence of being able to profit from such intensive-scale therapy. They may have been right, but I'll never know.

So it came to be that Susan was discharged to a subacute rehab facility within a nursing home. It had been about three and a half weeks since her first admission, and almost exactly three weeks in NYU.

What had caused all this, which was in fact a drastic decline in Susan's condition from the past several years? Her neurologist said gnomically, "It's the progression of her disease." Although his comment mystified me at the time (I thought, what disease?), I now think that was the simple truth. Her low sodium, which may have caused the seizures, and her fever, and everything that followed—all may have been caused by nothing but her brain not doing its proper work of organizing the various systems in her body. I had been fretting about a nasty cold virus Susan had after Christmas and about an antihistamine I had given her; I had quizzed the doctors repeatedly about whether Susan had suffered any subacute overnight seizures (once there seemed to be some); I was trying to piece together possible correlations between food or activity and seizures—my mind was searching in every little corner for a clue that might solve this puzzle, but in reality the cause of it all was right there directly in front of me: Susan's sadly wounded brain, gradually, gradually losing its power to hold her body together.

The Dark Night

Susan was discharged to a particular nursing home only because it was the first on our list of five to accept her. The social worker had pressured me to add more names to our list, and I had added this name on the slim basis of a stray comment someone had made. The social worker had assured me that we wouldn't have to take it. But when this institution said they could take Susan, it was instantly settled: she would go there, and go that evening.

This was about five o'clock. A transport ambulance was to pick Susan up shortly; it didn't arrive until after nine o'clock. It was nearly ten when Susan was admitted to the nursing home. It was hot and old; her room, painted an industrial shade of green, had three other beds that were at the moment empty. And the nurse seemed to hate people. I would later meet some people there who were kind and good to Susan. But there were many who weren't, and all of them seemed stressed and spread thin. Over the next weeks a loud buzzer seemed to go off interminably at the main desk on the floor, not far outside Susan's room, and the staff would ignore it; they had to do other things, and there weren't enough of them to respond to that awful noise. During future days I would find Susan's roommates—all the beds having been filled—each sitting in a wheelchair in front of her individual TV, each turned to high volume. Daytime television is hell—crude, vulgar, pathetic—but it is a worse hell to have multiple TVs going at once. I gave thanks once again that Susan never watched TV.

I told Susan's admitting nurse that she was hyponatremic and thus should not be given water. But, the nurse said, we give water with the feeds that go into the stomach, to clean the system. But,

I said, Susan might have a seizure if her sodium level goes down, and you may send it down by giving her that extra water. I didn't think she understood me. Because I was insistent, she phoned the doctor who had been assigned to oversee Susan's care, a doctor we had never met. The next day I would meet him, and we would walk the overheated stairs together (the whole building was over-heated); he was a decent man, an old doctor with a Park Avenue address. He had to lose his temper a few times, but it was finally established that, for Susan, whenever water was given to cleanse her feeding tube, it would be saline.

The nurse was brusque with me and seemed unhappy to have to admit Susan that evening. I was wretched myself. But I couldn't stay—not allowed. No one suggested I spend the night in case Susan woke up worried. I left with a packet of paperwork, and I wept as I rode the subway home.

What, I cried, what have I done to Susan? Why did I let this happen?

Being Heard

In every theology class I ever had, somewhere along the way it would be stated: human beings are social animals. Often, since my teachers were mostly leftists, this would be put forth as an attack on capitalism or the Republican Party. Christians are not individualists, and hence we cannot endorse an economic model that relies on individual self-interest. Instead, we should care about the common good and support proposals for additional government spending that often, by the way, happen to emanate from the Democratic Party.

Put so, our sociality is a highly contestable thesis. It is too political (in the partisan sense) and too shallow (in the philosophical sense). We are indeed social animals, but that reality is complex: it is thanks to our sociality that we are able to be individuals.

What I mean is that each of us begins our life in the middle of much else. In the normal run of things, we come from parents within families within neighborhoods within cities within larger societal groups. We are bound up with organizations like unions or social clubs or sports teams or musical groups or schools, and perhaps with many such organizations. We may well be connected with a church or other religious body. It is in the midst of all this sociality that individuals come to be. As Susan had written in the *Human Life Review*, communities make individuals.

And in turn, as individuals grow in the midst of their various communities, they shape and modify those communities by their own contributions to the common life. So not only do communities make individuals, but in turn individuals shape communities. Still, they do not originate them.

So the deeper Christian truth is that *both* (a) the community comes before the individual *and* (b) the individual is the point of the community.

There is an important corollary to this truth. To be an individual is to be heard by the community. A silenced individual is cut off from that which brought him to be. He cannot influence his community in turn. Thus things break down.

I was not being heard. Those months of Susan's hospitalization and then placement for rehabilitation in the nursing home were months in which my voice was often a cry in an empty desert. It was hard to get the effective attention of hospital staff. Apart from her time at the NYU hospital, I could not get a clear sense of who was responsible for Susan's care. When I did speak with someone, I was never sure that the result of our conversation would be communicated to all those who were involved with treating Susan. I saw, in both hospitals but particularly in the nursing home, that the staff were harried and that some of them did not like their jobs. I could not speak frankly with them, for fear that they might take it out on Susan.

Why do people pay lots of money to psychiatrists? In order to be heard.

And why, for that matter, did God send his Son to live a human life? In order to be not only the Word who speaks to us but also the Word who hears us.

And why do Christians pray "through Jesus Christ our Lord"? Because through Jesus God hears us.

If we aren't being heard, we aren't being human.

Recovery

Even the best of nursing homes are difficult places. Susan ended up being in hers for six weeks before she was discharged to home. A few times she had tried to get out of bed by herself and had fallen; no harm was done. But they would phone the news to me at the wrong number, despite repeated instructions to call my cell phone. That is just one of many instances of their frustrating bureaucratic ineptitude, their failure to hear me. Nonetheless, there were therapists who worked hard with Susan and loved her. They put her wheelchair in a place where she'd see other people and perhaps speak. They got her eating food again. They got her walking a bit—although, for most of the day, she was required and constrained to stay in her wheelchair.

Once I took Susan to the recreation floor and brought her close to the window. Here there were windows facing the southeast from about fifteen floors up. I helped her stand and protected her from falling by holding on to a loop at the back of her pants (as I had been taught by a therapist). We enjoyed the view of the Upper East Side and picked out some buildings we knew and other landmarks. But this therapeutic moment would not last. An employee came over and said she couldn't allow me to have Susan out of her chair. I protested: this is helpful to Susan, to stand and get used to putting weight on her legs. But no, it was not to be allowed.

When Susan came home, it was a very happy day. And immediately her recovery accelerated. She was again in pleasant and familiar surroundings. And she was not trapped in a wheelchair.

Anxiety

A couple of weeks before her discharge, I was participating in an ecumenical dialogue in New York City. It was my first meeting with the U.S. Anglican–Roman Catholic dialogue. The theological work of this dialogue was intrinsically interesting to me, and I would get to meet and work with some leading scholars in both our churches. It was also professionally validating: I had reached a point where I could contribute to the national Episcopal Church in a small yet significant way. At a reception at the end of the first day of dialogue, as we were about to go to dinner, I felt suddenly hot, with tingling in my arm and around my mouth. I stepped aside into our host's study and phoned my insurance company's advice nurse. Hearing my symptoms, she put me on hold for a minute, then came back and asked if someone there could take me to an emergency room. She didn't say, but I suspected she thought I might be having a heart attack; I presumed she didn't say so explicitly lest it agitate me. In the emergency room they quickly ruled out a heart attack, did another test or two, waited for the results, and everything seemed fine. In due course the doctor came to speak to me. He asked if I had changed any medications lately or if there was anything different in my life. No, I said, medications are few and unchanged, and my life is fine. Well, I added, actually, my wife was in the hospital for most of January and now she's in a nursing home. And I started crying. I couldn't speak.

O gentle physician! How lovingly you then spoke to me! A bit later, you gave me a dose of Valium. You called my own doctor, who said to phone the next day and come see him the day after that.

I had thought I was doing so well! I was continuing to do the essential work at church. I was encouraging many people to visit Susan, and I was keeping on top of all the things being done with and for her, being actively involved as her voice and advocate in the complexities of her nursing home care. I was taking care of my body, exercising at the gym every other day and walking briskly even on subway stairs. I was keeping up with church, preaching and teaching, saying masses, doing the office work I had to do, staying on top of it all. Everything is just fine! I can handle this!

And my body spoke. Not so, it said.

What the Body Knows

Saint Luke tells us about a complex healing scene involving Jesus. A prominent Jewish man, "Jairus by name," falls down before Jesus and begs him to come to his home and heal his daughter who is at the point of death. Without any delay, indeed without any discussion, Jesus immediately takes off with the man to go to his house. But there is a large crowd with Jesus, and it is through the crowd that Jesus and Jairus are pressing when a woman comes into the picture. Unnoticed by anyone else, this woman has had a flow of blood for a dozen years and has spent all her money on physicians, but nothing has done any good. She has figured out that Jesus' body itself has the power to heal, and that somehow his healing power radiates out from his body. So she has said to herself that she need only touch his garment and she will be healed. She is in the crowd, Jesus is close, and she touches his garment from behind. Just as she expected: immediately she is healed.

Jesus asks who has touched him—a question that seems quite odd to his disciples, since there is a vast crowd of people all pressing upon him. Lots of people have touched you! What can you mean? Jesus means that he has felt power go out from him. He looks around. The woman acknowledges that she touched him. She is healed, and Jesus affirms her faith.

By this time, Jesus having been delayed in the crowd, the little girl has died. Jesus nonetheless goes to her and restores her to life. And there is great rejoicing all around (Luke 8:41–56).

Reader, focus back on that moment in the crowd right after the woman has touched Jesus. She has been instantly healed; indeed, she is healed before Jesus notices her or attends to her in any way. Jesus hasn't thought anything. He has not spoken; he has not reached out his hands to touch; he has engaged neither his mind nor his will. There is just *something in his body*, a power in his body, and that power was exercised *before Jesus knew it or willed it*. In this case, *Jesus' body "knew" something before his mind thought it.*

The human body shares in the intelligence and the volition of the human person. Our intellect and will are not located specifically in our brains. After all, our brains are just part of our body, and our soul (or, if you wish, our "mind") is not the same thing as our brain. Our soul is our "livingness," and it is intimately united with our body as a whole. And in extreme cases, our bodies can know something before it comes to the attention of our conscious intellect or actual will.

My body knew something that I was not conscious of. Once I left the emergency room, it was clear. I was afraid Susan would never come home. I was afraid that the status quo of the past ten or fifteen years had been lost, that she would have to be institutionalized and would never get better. I was also apprehensive about what this would mean for my life. My world, which I thought of as solid, and in which I thought I was working so well, was in fact like one of those dream rooms where you go to lean against a wall and discover it's just tissue paper. The wall gives way, and you start to fall, and nothing stops you from falling; you just keep going down. If I was refusing to see these things with my mind—and I was—well, my body was going to assert its own knowledge.

While this is an awful thing, it carries within it something awesome. My body can have its own knowledge, just as Jesus' body did. And while mine told me of the awful depletion of my strength, Jesus' body irradiated the strength of his healing power. In each case, something was going out, and in each case, we knew it after the fact.

Blessed Speech Therapists

The hospitalization and rehab period of January and February 2012, grim as it was, had, to call on the overused image, a silver lining. This came out of Susan's need to relearn how to swallow safely without aspirating food or liquid into her lungs. It was fear of such aspiration that had caused the feeding tube to be surgically implanted in her stomach in the first place. Now, to our delight, we found that the professionals who teach how to swallow are speech therapists.

Over the years Susan's voice, which was never brash or forceful, had diminished to near inaudibility. Not only was it hard for Susan to formulate words—one of the more direct consequences of her progressing brain disease—but she lacked the volume to be heard. We could be talking with someone—a waiter, say, at a restaurant—and she would think she had said something to him. "He can't hear you," I'd say, not always with gentleness. I think she processed what I was saying, but she wasn't capable of remembering it for the next time.

Beginning in the nursing home and continuing for several months thereafter, Susan received speech therapy. All of us who cared for Susan came to admire these therapists particularly. They were loving and urgent at the same time and gave her exercises that were puzzles for her mind as well as her body. A simple exercise was to count from one to five, with each number being louder: "one" was very quiet (Susan's normal voice) and "five" was to be shouted so loud that the neighbors could hear it. Susan discovered that she could sit a bit straighter, breathe in deeply, and lay claim to a loud voice.

It became a bit of a game. I told people at church. They'd go up to her in her chair at coffee hour and say, "Susan, I hear that you have a loud voice." She'd beam a smile bright enough to melt ice, breathe in, and say, "YES!" And she could indeed be heard, although perhaps not really across the hall, at least from one person to another.

Speech therapists work at a particular junction of intellect and body that proved personally helpful to Susan. In terms of her ability to find words, to communicate audibly, and to stay focused on a thought long enough to give expression to it, she was better off in the middle of 2012 than she had been for several years. Despite the terrible setbacks, this was a blessing.

Her speech therapist at the Rusk Institute—to which she was finally admitted as an outpatient—encouraged her also to sing, and encouraged me to sing with her. Our morning routine in those months at home was for me to awaken her at seven o'clock and to assist her safely to the toilet. While she sat there, I took my shower, and we'd sing songs like "Oh, what a beautiful morning" from *Oklahoma*, and "It's a good day for singing a song" from we didn't know where, and "It's a jolly holiday with Mary" from *Mary Poppins*. After my shower, I would help her into the shower, and then, while she held the rail, I would wash her. She improved remarkably over those months. While I wished then (and still do) that we had made use of speech therapy years earlier, I gave thanks for the speech therapists that she had. They are among the most blessed beings on our planet. May God, whose Word spoke with lungs and vocal cords, prosper them all. (One of them, Karen, was at Susan's funeral; I glimpsed her as we walked out at the end.)

The Happy Return to October; Its Tragic End

By the end of that summer Susan was doing so well that she was discharged from all outpatient rehabilitation. We had a sign or two of internal fragility, one of which happened on a very hot day when I tried to get her to walk a few blocks too far. Her brain didn't control her body temperature (she was flushing red), and instead of just calling a taxi, I had the crazy idea of getting to a nearby Starbucks and cooling off with a special drink. Susan would have enjoyed that drink, but when we got to Starbucks she collapsed and cut her cheek on the corner of a table.

Even then, what kindness we saw. A woman stepped forward from the crowd that had surrounded us and announced she was a nurse on vacation from Australia. She dabbed Susan's cut with a napkin soaked in ice water and held her hand and comforted her. Susan was conscious throughout this. The nurse asked the Starbucks employee if they had any "plasters"—he said no, and I didn't think until later that we probably should have translated this Britishism for "Band-Aids." Susan revived and quite emphatically declined going to a hospital. We got a taxi home.

Yet despite these occasional signs, those were, overall, beautiful months. Susan enjoyed better relations with other people, and she had significantly more interactions. We had new friends who had volunteered to come and be with Susan whenever we needed that. In March and April it had been important that Susan not be left alone. And it continued to be very helpful for her to have to talk with different people and do her various physical and speech exercises with them. Even after she had improved enough that she could be alone, at least for short periods, it was still good for her to have friends who visited regularly. This was another thing that I wished we had done earlier—another silver lining.

And it was still possible for the two of us to communicate with lucidity and from the heart. There was one evening that summer—we were lying together in bed, and I spoke deliberately and Susan grasped my meaning. I told her I was glad for everything she was and everything she had given me. She had loved me and I would never regret marrying her, and I would be with her to the end, whatever happened. By grace I was able to say that which I too often did not say. And I remember: I was able to speak clearly, and she understood. I was glad to have her now just as much as then. I stroked her head, with its scars and the problems beneath. Her head was dear under my hand, her soul dear all over. With that clarity, we then slept.

Reader, please note there are three characters in that last paragraph: two that you see, and one who undergirds it and whose presence is marked by the prepositional phrase "by grace."

Susan's recovery reached its apex when we flew to Phoenix in October. We stayed there a week again, just like the previous year. My parents drove out to be with us, and my brother and his wife came down from Denver. There is a picture of all of us together, including two grandchildren and a third quite obviously in utero. Susan is standing, leaning on her cane, wearing a straw hat, grinning with joy. Just the previous year our trip to Phoenix had been marred by her grand mal seizure on the last day. This time there were no seizures. There was only the joy of being together in love.

And then the end began.

We had been home for a day when Susan fell on the way to the bathroom. It happened like this: She had been taking her nap when I found her standing beside the bed, incontinent. I urged her to get moving, to move faster. I went ahead to get the toilet ready for her—when I heard it. She had pivoted on one foot and fallen backwards, her head loudly thunking on a closet door. I found her on her back on the floor, her head up against the door. She was awake, she wasn't bleeding, and she could speak; I helped her stand, and we continued to the toilet. But while seated there, she became unresponsive. She didn't reply to anything I said. Her head was turned away from me to the wall; her focus was on the toilet paper. She put a hand to the paper. She sat. She didn't reply.

(It can still haunt my memory. Why did she fall? Why wasn't I with her?)

When the ambulance arrived, her seizure was over, and the drivers would not take her to the NYU hospital but insisted on going elsewhere, to yet another hospital, one at which Susan would be a patient without previous medical records and with an unknown history, apart from what I could verbally communicate. At this hospital it was thought that she might have had a heart event or a stroke, which I couldn't deny was a theoretical possibility. In two days, her heart tests all being negative, Susan was better and released to home. If only the ambulance had taken her to NYU, if only at that time an MRI had been done of her brain, what might have been found? When the next week her neurologist saw her, he said to get an MRI just to make sure nothing was wrong. He said that to us calmly, but I heard him say to the scheduler that it should be done "ASAP."

The day of the MRI was the last day Susan spoke a word. It began with physical therapy at home (because of the hospital visit, she had been reauthorized for home therapy). Susan was tired from that, and the friend who was with her that morning told me, when I came home shortly after noon, that they had eaten an early lunch and Susan had gone down for her nap. I woke her up later, and we got into a cab to go to the hospital, where the MRI equipment was. Susan was moving slowly. We had a four o'clock appointment. I was afraid we'd be late. "Can't you walk a little faster?" I was cross.

We checked in for the appointment and then sat down to wait. Rather, I sat down; Susan was just being slow, and I thought that if I left her at the desk she would see her way to come sit by me. She finally did.

They were running very much behind schedule. Susan kept falling asleep in the chair in an uncomfortable posture, leaning over herself. Around five o'clock I told the clerk my wife was exceedingly tired and asked if she might lie down somewhere while we waited. They were accommodating and put her on a stretcher in a back room. At last she was taken for the MRI. Afterwards, with Susan reclining again on that stretcher, we had to wait for a neurosurgeon intern to come and reprogram her shunt. When that was finally over, I sat beside Susan, holding her; she was hardly responding to anything. The stretcher lost its balance, and we ended up on the floor. Someone came in and helped us get up, and then a nurse came in to check Susan. There seemed to be no harm, just this strangeness that she wasn't being responsive. Since it was now eight in the evening, we really wanted to go home—so they offered us a wheelchair to take to the street for a taxi.

I had Susan in the wheelchair, and we were crossing the largely empty lobby. It occurred to me that her problems with slowness might have to do with lack of food, but the Argo Tea shop (where we could have gotten a salad or a muffin) was now closed. I got a package of peanut M&Ms from a vending machine. I gave Susan a couple. I don't remember if she put them in her mouth, or if I did. She smiled at me. I was sitting in a chair facing her in her wheelchair. "You have M&Ms in your mouth," I said. She smiled. "Don't you want to swallow them?" I said. She smiled.

It dawned on me that, on the other side of this hospital complex, there was an emergency room. I hated the thought of not going home, but it seemed prudent at least to call Susan's neurologist before we left.

The attending doctor called me back in just a few minutes. Grasping the essential ambiguity of the situation, he said we could either go home or go to the ER to have her checked out.

I chose the ER.

It was nine o'clock. A crowded scene: Susan on a bed, with curtains separating her from others, and with hardly room to stand on either side. Many people checked her various bodily signs. She still was looking with her eyes, but her head was turned to one side only. If I stood on the other side of the bed, she would not turn to me. If I was on the side of the bed she was looking at, she seemed to see me.

About midnight she was admitted to a room on the neurological floor, and I went home.

That was the last day she ever spoke to me. The last day she squeezed my hand. The last day she sat beside me. The last day I sat beside her with my arm around her shoulders. The last day she put weight on her feet. The last day she put food in her mouth.

I will not hide my shame from my readers, or my regret. It was the last day I was ever cross with her.

It is such a trite observation: you never know which day will be the last day. Yet even though trite, it is true. And it would be nearly two months still before I would realize that, in all those ways, for all those quotidian things, this was the last day.

The Best Book in the Bible

When God gave Susan and me to each other in marriage, I discovered that enfleshed human desire could be enjoyed without any distancing from the love of God. Because it draws us into this truth, the Song of Songs is a great book of the Bible; indeed, I have called it the second greatest of the biblical books.

But even though God gave me my heart's desire, and even though the love of Susan (a person I could touch and embrace and speak to and have unbounded intercourse with) was delightfully intertwined with the love of God, it remains the case that the God I love, the God who loves me, is strange. However intimate he may be with us, and however great the intimacies he gives to us, he is himself always an Other, the Mystery behind existence, whose oddness can never be mastered.

And that's why the greatest book of the Bible is the book of Job. It is not an easy book to read; a bored boy in church is not going to pick it up for diversion. It has no beauty of the flesh, and it does not raise the heartbeat with ravishing descriptions of the body of one's lover. It is a book whose truth is handed over only to a careful reader. Indeed, it seems a person must go through considerable suffering before he or she can begin to understand it.

For decades I thought that I got the broad point of the book of Job, and I thought its broad point rather trivial. Job starts out a rich man. He loses all his possessions, his children, and his own health. His friends come and tell him that he must have sinned because, according to their theology, people who are horribly afflicted are that way because God is punishing them for something. Job replies that he is innocent of wrongdoing, and thus God can't be punishing him. Job's friends and he go back and forth with pointless repetitions (so I thought) of the same immovable claims, them saying that anyone afflicted like Job must have sinned, Job saying that it ain't so. Finally God speaks, but he doesn't answer any of the questions of the book. God shows Job that the universe is vast and awesome and frightening to humans. Finally Job gets back his health, his children, and even more goods than he had at the beginning.

The point of the book seemed trivial and its details tedious. What is the reader to make of it all? The entire book, one might reckon, could be summarized in a single sentence: "I'm God and you're not"—as indeed a professor at seminary once put it. To be sure, that blunt insistence on the otherness of God is one way to answer the problem of evil: human beings are not in a position to put God in the dock. We simply cannot ask the question; even if we think we're asking the question, we fail to do so, because God is not the sort of being who can be held to any standard of behavior. There is no place of moral rectitude that is independent of God, and no standard of morality that can be put over God. To put it slightly provocatively, it doesn't make sense to speak of God as being "morally well-behaved," as if he were acting in accordance with what a god *ought* to do.

And while I agree wholeheartedly that God is a very strange being, and while I believe he was and is mysteriously with me through every page of this book in your hands and every aspect of my life with Susan, still there is more wisdom to be plumbed in the book of Job than I thought for all those years.

One needs to start by looking at the text itself, looking closely, and trusting that the text has something to say.

First, while it is obvious that the book seems to have the structure of a sandwich, with (as St. John's College tutor Robert Sacks puts it) simple Dick-and-Jane style writing in the opening and closing chapters while in the middle there is poetry of high elegance, we will do well to take the entire book seriously as one book. Let us resist taking the beginning and the end as a primitive tale into the middle of which a lot of boring and repetitive speechifying has been placed. For one thing, the speeches of Job's friends and his replies, which go through almost three rounds, are in fact not simply repetitive. For another, God's reply to Job is significantly related to some of the themes of those speeches. But most fundamentally, the so-called primitive opening and closing are themselves far from naive.

Consider the following: In chapter 1 we are told that Job had seven sons and three daughters. At the end of the book we are told that "the LORD blessed the latter days of Job more than his beginning" and that, along with thousands of animals, Job "had also seven sons and three daughters" (42:12–13). But at the end of the book, unlike at the beginning, the daughters are given names. The daughters and the sons at the beginning were not named, and the sons at the end are not named—but the daughters have names. And not just names: the daughters at the end have an inheritance right along with their brothers. And that announcement about the inheritance Job gave to his daughters is the last thing that is said in the book of Job, save that Job lived a long time and finally died.

With patient reading, then, one comes to see that something of great importance must have happened to Job in the course of the book, something that ultimately causes Job to name his daughters and include them in the inheritance. What is it?

It is, in part, a clarification of how to speak of his predicament that comes through the dialectic with his friends. This clarification could be stated in terms of the difference between the surface world and the deep structure of reality. In the surface world unjust things happen to people (including righteous Job), but the deep structure is supposed to be one of justice. How do we reconcile the surface to what is beneath? But then one comes to see that there is not just one surface world; there are many. The customs of one place, its safeties and dangers and the wrongs that occur in it, are not exactly the same as those in another. And outside the perimeter of the human world there is an untamed world, a world unknown to humans. Might justice be found there also? Job, in fact, longs to go out there, to take, we might say with a bit of orneriness, a walk on the wild side.

And God invites him.

God invites Job—his speech is polite, a "please" could be put in the translation, "Please gird up your loins like a man" (38:3, repeated at 40:7)—to come out and see the world he has made. "Have you ever come upon the source of the seas, or gone for a walk down by the cranny in the deep?" (38:16 Sacks). God's intent seems to be, in part, to reveal the universe as having existence and purpose beyond its use to human beings. In a way, the book of Job slightly corrects the book of Genesis. There, in the first chapter of the Bible, it is emphasized that sun and moon are creations of God and not themselves divine. Their point is to mark days and seasons, all ultimately for the human being, who is the culmination of creation. But here, Job sees the Pleiades and Orion as simply awesome, nonhuman, beyond human comprehension, existing without any human regard (see 38:31–33). In chapter 39, Job is shown six kinds of wild beasts. They are all beasts known to him, but they are shown to him in their strangeness. They do not need him to exist; many of them could destroy him and not pause to think about it.

One of them, the ostrich, is shown rather humorously. She leaves her eggs in the dust, and whether they hatch or not is no concern of hers. God made her that way, a way that, in the human world, would be immoral. But Job is not in the human world.

"Please gird up your loins"—and become a man! Finally Job sees the Behemoth (chap. 40), who is huge, frightening, and impenetrable. The point is made that he has a hide that is completely covered with scales; nothing can get in. And here, one might well think, Job begins to understand something. Job does not have an impenetrable hide. Job's skin, in fact, is precisely what was afflicted at the beginning. Satan, the great skeptic of claims of righteousness, had suggested that Job's righteousness was only skin-deep. He was proved wrong.

Job cannot live, no human being can live, outside the human world that God has made for us. But Job can bring back to that human world the priceless gift of understanding, a gift won through suffering and integrity. When, in the final chapter, Job has been restored to a condition of health and prosperity, when God has given him new children, his neighbors come to him to console him. This time, unlike at the beginning, they are able to console him. I think they can console him because he has been changed. Something from the wild world has been brought into the human world, and now human companionship is possible. And it is possible not because everything is happy on the surface. Here the text is unstintingly honest. It is a verse that should be memorized by every human being.

> Then came to him all his brothers and sisters and all who had known him before, and ate bread with him in his house; and they showed him sympathy and comforted him for all the evil that the LORD had brought upon him. (42:11)

There is human fellowship, yes; there is the achievement of communion, yes; but do not overlook those stark words: *all the evil that the LORD had brought upon him.*

I have not yet plumbed to the bottom the mysteries of the book of Job—to do so, I think, one must be able to hear Jesus' cry from the cross—yet even now this much seems clear and true. We need not be afraid of speaking truthfully about the gifts God has given us. And to speak truthfully means being willing to say, bluntly, that he has taken those gifts away, that, in doing so, he has brought evils upon us. If we can say that, then it becomes possible for comfort to be given and communion to be shared. It becomes possible, furthermore, for us to recognize the dignity of other people and, perhaps, make an adjustment to our wills and testaments.

Although she had several weeks yet to live, Susan would never speak to me again. For most of that time she would not respond in any way we could perceive to anything going on around her. God, who had given us so much, now gave us this evil.

Sandy

The NYU doctors were perplexed by Susan's condition. A fever was measured, so they feared that an unknown infection was causing or contributing to her problem. Many things were checked. There was a tap of her spinal fluid, drawn from the reservoir of her brain shunt. (The intern doing that didn't find it an easy task, and I hoped he wasn't aggravating Susan's problems.) Blood tests also were done. In the lab, attempts were being made to grow cultures in her extracted spinal fluid; they would take several days. In the meantime, antibiotics were being given. A continuous EEG was being run on Susan. Visitors came; doctors came. We all tried to talk with her. We stroked her feet and held her hand. We hopefully interpreted her twitches as signs of her coming back to herself, signs of responsiveness to the outside world.

A few days passed. On Sunday afternoon, two neurologists were reviewing Susan's EEG, wondering if she was having continuous seizures. I had to leave them because I was preaching at Evensong at church. That night, superstorm Sandy hit New York City.

As the storm came through on Monday, I didn't venture out to the hospital. The city wanted everyone to stay indoors, and I certainly didn't want to be hit by flying debris and become a patient alongside Susan. I thought about and prayed for her through the day.

In the evening I phoned the nurses' station, but no one picked up. I figured everyone in New York was phoning for information, and they needed to focus on their patients.

I slept through the news of the hospital's power failure and evacuation.

My colleague, whose baby was born that night at NYU, sent me a text with the news that he had been evacuated to Mount Sinai and that he assumed Susan was there too, but that no one would give him information.

Tuesday morning I phoned Mount Sinai. Susan was not there. Where was she? The receptionist at Mount Sinai named five other hospitals where Susan might be.

After several confused phone calls, I learned that she was at a hospital close to our home. She was back at the hospital where she had been taken at the beginning of the year. I walked there and found her in the ICU. A veritable team of medical people were quite glad to see me.

Because: Susan had arrived with only a brief printout of information about her. When the power went out at NYU, so did access to all electronic records. (And, of course, all the cultures being grown in the lab were lost. Also her MRIs, her EEGs—everything of that sort was inaccessible.) The people at the hospital didn't know she had a husband. They certainly didn't know my phone number. Yes, they were glad to see me.

One of my memories of that poststorm morning is of a gruff, no-nonsense man who tried shouting at Susan to awaken her. He and others throughout the day also tried running things over the soles of her feet. They resumed her IV medicines, ordered tests, asked me to bring the CT scan from three weeks previous that I had at home. (I kicked myself for not having insisted on a CD of the MRI of the previous week.)

What Is It?

A day or two later, I was sitting beside her bed, staying to the side of the camera that was always on Susan (the camera was part of the video EEG). Maybe I was talking to her, maybe I was praying, maybe I was checking email on my Palm. But I saw it: her lips were moving. "Susie, your lips are moving! Are you trying to say something?" I rushed toward her, tears in my eyes, with all the hopes in the world that what I most wanted of all God was giving to me. "Susie! What are you trying to say?"

And then she started seizing: the heavy breathing, the bodily convulsions. I shouted for help. They gave her an injection of Ativan. Her seizure stopped; her body relaxed.

Her lips became still.

The Kidneys Have Their Say

Susan was in ICU nearly a month, unresponsive. There were a variety of hypotheses about infections, none of them ever clearly proven. A pushy neurologist got me to agree to put her into an induced coma. This is standard procedure when *status epilepticus* is presumed. I call this neurologist "pushy" because she made that diagnosis before talking to me or learning anything of Susan's history. She never, for instance, contacted Susan's neurologist who had taken care of her since 2005. My consent to the induced coma is a decision that I have often second-guessed.

Yet I tell myself the obvious things: Susan had been ill for a long time. Her brain was gradually losing its ability to run her body. I think, now, that at least some of the fevers that were measured during her hospitalization were not caused by any outside thing or infection but were simply manifestations of her brain not being able to control her body temperature. I think, too, that she wasn't in her then-existing condition because of continuous seizures but rather because of her brain's weakness (although the two are perhaps not mutually exclusive).

Susan's previous PEG—the feeding tube in her stomach—had been removed over the summer after she relearned to swallow and no longer needed it. Now back in a hospital, she was again receiving nutrition through a nasal tube. To protect her nasal tissue, and for the induced coma, a new PEG had to be installed. Indeed, she might also have been feeling discomfort from the nasal tube, which would be real discomfort even if she couldn't express it to us. More drastically, the induced coma required that she also have a tracheotomy.

After the coma, as the medicines were gradually reduced, the doctors were satisfied that she wasn't having seizures. In due course she was moved out of the ICU to the neurological floor.

About this time, her blood tests began to show problems with the sodium levels. A test was done of her kidney function and showed it to be fine. The intern told me it was something he had studied but never seen before: "cerebral salt wastage." Normally, if a person's salt level is low, it's because the kidneys aren't doing their work. But in Susan's case, it was because her brain wasn't giving the right signals to her kidneys.

I absorbed the datum: another sign of her brain not working.

Crossing Another Line

As with Susan's first stay at this hospital at the beginning of 2012, so now with her last months there, I had problems with continuity of communication. Even though I now understood it to be a teaching institution with various doctors continually rotating through, I still had to work hard to learn, on any given day, to whom I should try to speak about Susan's care. There was, however, Dr. Wolf, who happened onto Susan when she first arrived, who established communication with her NYU neurologist, and who communicated almost daily with me. I got the sense that what he was doing was slightly irregular—the pushy neurologist, mentioned earlier, spoke to me of her frustration of having to defer to him as a "*pediatric* neurologist" (her scornful emphasis). But I was grateful that he saw my need and cared for Susan.

I wanted to talk with him in person about Susan's overall condition, so I phoned him—I had his cell number; it is a sign of his care that he had given it to me the first day. It was now late November. He said he'd be in Susan's room around eight the next morning. I excused myself from the parish's vestry meeting in order to see him.

Susan at this point was still in ICU. She had gone through the induced coma and come out. Her medical care was presently aimed at defeating various possible infections, trying to lower her anticonvulsant medicines so that she might become responsive, and also weaning her off the ventilator. I alluded to these various things and asked him my real question, the question from my heart. "At what point should we start to think about a do-not-resuscitate order?"

Not missing a beat, he said, "Now."

Later that day the head ICU doctor spoke with me and explained that to sign such an order would in no way reduce the level of care Susan would receive. "We will continue to do everything we would otherwise do," he said, "except that, if her heart stops, we will not try to bring it back."

I knew from my pastoral training that resuscitation can be a harsh procedure upon any human body. And, much as I didn't want to have Susan die, I even more did not want her body so assaulted—her weakened, ventilated, long-suffering, beautiful body.

That night I phoned each of our children to talk it over. I was careful to say that this was my decision, not theirs: I did not want to lay upon them any grounds for future regret; I did not want to lay this burden upon them. But I also wanted them to understand, and I wanted their counsel. We agreed, and the next day I signed the order.

So Susan had a new wristband: DNR.

Tears and Hope

Michael was torn about whether to fly in from Phoenix for a visit; he would have to leave his wife, Melissa, behind, for she was too far advanced in her third pregnancy to fly, and with her he would have to leave their children. But to both Emily and me, Susan's situation seemed grave enough to urge a visit. Once he arrived, we were all together to meet with the neurologist who had been my continuing line of communication. While we were in the room with their mother, we began to notice: Susan seemed to be looking at us. Michael went up to one side of her bed, and she looked at him. He went to the other side, and she turned her eyes (not her head) towards him.

Dr. Wolf was amazed. Silently and without response, Susan was watching us talking together. He saw it as an unexpected and hopeful sign of the possibility of recovery.

We have a picture of Michael and Emily leaning over the hospital bed and Susan looking at them. She doesn't react, doesn't smile; she has the trach in her throat, IVs going into her arm for medicines, the PEG in her stomach for food; she doesn't squeeze her hand or move her toes or do anything except: her eyes stay focused on them. I don't think she was able to turn her head, but my memory may be incomplete. Her eyes stay focused. She is definitely looking at them. They are saying to her, We love you, Mama. They are reading to her the sonnet by Gerard Manley

Hopkins that begins, "The world is charged with the grandeur of God," a favorite poem by a favorite poet. They are reading to her about the splendor and glory of God and the universe. They are reading it over and over because they want to memorize it. Her eyes move. She is clearly taking it in.

And then more: Emily remembers her making "a hilarious face, as if we were torturing her with our inability to memorize the poem." Her face, of course, could have meant nothing but that she liked the poem, or wanted to speak, "but she was really grimacing, and Michael and I kept laughing."

And then more: I discovered that she was beginning to recover control over her body. She was able to pucker her lips.

She kissed me.

Every day as I went in to see her, I would speak from the moment of entry, talking as I put down my pack and took off my coat, walking over to her, slipping my fingers into her hand, stroking her hair (what little of it remained after weeks of EEG monitors being glued into the scalp under her thin hair), leaning over to smile at her, and so slowly lowering my lips to hers. Her lips rose up to meet mine.

She was able to kiss me.

After the strange withdrawal back in October when we went for the MRI and did not return home from the hospital; after the near-hurricane that took out the hospital's power; after being alone, by herself, and then the darkness of the evacuation as she was carried down unending flights of stairs and doubtless jarred and disoriented and totally noncommunicative; after a month of ICU and the induced coma; after weeks of near-weaning from the ventilator; after a variety of antibiotics and a succession of fevers that came and went; even now still receiving medicines and sodium and other mineral supplements from day to day; after nearly two months of this and more: Susan was manifestly aware of her surroundings.

There followed a glorious, happy week. Many visitors from church came and remarked how changed she was. The hospital began to prepare me for her discharge. I started to check out nursing homes for what just possibly might be long-term rehab rather than a permanent placement. On Friday, I visited three homes. In the evening I returned to the hospital, my notes say, for three hours. I wrote this: "S opened eyes and was very present. Lots of attempted smiles. Can move her tongue around all her teeth and even a bit of sticking it out. Slight movement of head from side to side. At one point I thought she slightly squeezed her left hand on mine. When [I was] moving her left foot/shoe, her left hip/thigh seemed to twitch. Twitching also on her face; closing her eyes in a squeeze when I put on or remove [her] glasses (as [if] to protect herself); wincing when I picked at some sleep near her eye. Lots of kisses too."

My calendar has no notes from a visit on Saturday. I heard a confession at church and participated in a service at four in the afternoon. I also must have prepared a sermon, because I preached the next day at Evensong. But I probably visited in the morning or the evening, or both.

Sunday at church I was telling everyone how much better Susan was, and there was great rejoicing. After the church school Christmas pageant, which was at one in the afternoon, I was able to have a short visit with Susan before returning to preach. In a dramatic change, she was not well. My notes read: "About noon [Susan] had respiratory distress: high breathing rate. They put the vent back on her, gave her Ativan (2mg) and morphine (2mg). At 2:30 I see her red on face shoulders upper chest and arms somewhat, very hot to touch. Nurse says there hasn't been fever. Na is 136. Temp @ 3p is 99.9." After preaching, I was at home eating supper when the doctor called. He told me Susan had a fever, and they feared it might be caused by a pulmonary embolism. They wanted my consent to do a CT exam with an injection to see if there was a blood clot in her lungs. He also said the fever might be caused by an infection elsewhere. Susan was getting an antibiotic, again, for that possibility. I gave consent, and by the time I arrived Susan was out of the room for a test, the doctors with her. She returned, I don't recall how much later. I sat with her for a while, but, on the ventilator, feverish, flushed, she was not responsive. I held her hand. I talked a little and was silent a lot. I'm sure I tried to kiss her; I don't recall if she still had that response.

Back in early November, when they put the trach in her throat, I prayed over her, stroking her forehead, getting my mouth down close to her ear, telling her it was all okay. I repeated that again and again: it is okay; it is going to be okay. Then what I was saying turned into what Julian of Norwich prayed, lines we loved from the beginning of our marriage, lines used by Eliot near the end of "Little Gidding": all shall be well, all shall be well, all manner of thing shall be well. I didn't know, don't know, if she heard me. And then I inhaled deeply, and I prayed into Susan's ear: "Now I lay me down to sleep. I pray the Lord my soul to keep. If I die before I wake, I pray the Lord my soul to take."

It is hard to pray that final sentence. My intention, which was deeper than my fears and stronger than my quivering body, was to let Susan know that, if this was the end, it was okay.

Did I pray that prayer before I left her on Sunday, December 16, 2012? I do not recall. I do not think so. Although I had prayed it often at the end of the day with her when I was leaving her for the night, the past week had been so full of hope and promise that I don't think it even came to my mind, not even in the presence of her current distress.

She was calm, although flushed and on the ventilator. Tests had been done. I was hopeful that this would be just a bump in the road. I was ready to move forward.

I also knew it would be hard to have Susan in a nursing home. She might never recover enough to live at home, or it might take many months. I was prepared for that, prepared to accept that challenge if it came to me. It also might cost a lot of money, and I was prepared for that as well. What had we saved our money for, over the years, if not just for this? I didn't realize, that evening, that I was leaving her for the last time. For me, that evening—as for most of the previous nineteen years and six months and twelve days since that June 4 of 1993, when her tumor was found—that evening was a moment in the present that had an uncertain future stretching before it. I had courage and hope and knowledge from experience that, whatever happened, God would be with me to help me deal with it, and there would be friends to share the load and parishioners to pray with and for me. Again and again, that is what had happened. I didn't feel personally strong, nor did I presume that I could handle these things on my own. It was, rather: I'll take a deep breath; I'll take reasonable care of myself; I will be supported; we can carry on with this. In short, it was a sad day of a setback, but I did not think it was the last day.

December 17, 2012

I was eating cereal when the text message came from Dr. Wolf's assistant. It said: "Your wife doesn't look good this morning. Call when you get to the hospital."

I finished breakfast, filled my backpack with what I needed for the day (I was to give a final exam to a Fordham theology class that evening, and I planned to finish writing it at the hospital). I got there a bit after nine. I walked into Susan's room. "Dear Susie," I said to her, "your face isn't red like yesterday; you look much better." I put down my backpack and piled my coat on a chair and sterilized my hands. I went up to her and stroked her right arm, her face. "You aren't red like yesterday. You seem very calm." I looked at the monitors; I looked some more at her. Her eyes looked dry. I thought it bizarre, but it occurred to me that a dead person's eyes are dry, yet I didn't connect. I touched her eyelids. She didn't respond; she kept breathing calmly. I went around to the other side of the bed. I phoned the doctor who had kindly sent me the text, to say I was there. Just then the resident arrived.

I was apologizing for phoning another doctor, explaining about the text and noting that Susan's fever seemed to be over and that she was breathing without distress, when he started apologizing to me. "The nurse came to me, but I wasn't able to get here until now," he said.

What?

"Your wife died a few minutes ago."

She looked alive to me because of the ventilator. But she had no fever. And, now I knew, no heartbeat.

He asked me what I wanted to do, and I realized it was something I hadn't done since October. "I just want to get up in the bed beside her," I said.

"Of course," he replied, "let me remove some things." He disconnected the IVs, the feeding tube. He turned off the ventilator. In the background, our Gregorian chant CD was playing quietly—I had bought a CD player for Susan's room so that she could have quiet music near her that might soothe her soul and assist her brain's recovery. The chant CD was on a loop, just as I had left it the night before. With that music in the background and the ventilator now silenced, the doctor pulled the curtain and told me to take all the time I wanted. Not even removing my shoes, I got up beside Susan. I put my right arm under her head, my left across her body, my legs up as close as I gently could, my face up to her hair.

I wept. I spoke to her. I prayed as best I could from memory. *Depart O Christian soul out of this world, in the name of God the Father who created you, in the name of God the Son* . . . I was not convulsing. I was not violently sad. I was not thinking, then, of what might have been. (What if I had spent the night? What if I had arrived earlier? What if, what if, what if?)

There were no what-ifs. There was instead a perfectly natural yet immense sense of awe.

Love. The flesh of my bride in my arms.

Holiness. God suffusing this human moment with himself.

May She Rest

I had to call the church. It was Monday; of the clergy, only Joel would be in. I told him the news. I asked him to take the 12:10 mass for me.

Joel came right over to the hospital. We hugged and we prayed. He got me coffee. I asked if he might be able to administer the final exam for me. Of course he would be able to do so.

I don't remember the order of things. I phoned Emily. I phoned Melissa—Michael had already gone to work—and she burst into tears over the phone. I phoned my parents. I phoned Bridget, Susan's eldest sister, who then phoned her other sisters. I phoned my brother.

Another priest colleague, Michael, got the news at home and immediately came over to the hospital. David, a friend from church who had also helped care for Susan, came at the same time; they passed Joel on the street.

The rector phoned with his sympathy and love. He asked about a service for Susan. I said that we just wanted "The Burial of the Dead" from the Book of Common Prayer, with the Eucharist, and singing "The strife is o'er." Everything else, I said, was up to him. I knew he would do everything in good order; he had and has my complete trust and admiration. Later he called back and said that John Scott, our director of music, had offered Fauré's Requiem and that the full choir of men and boys would sing. I was stunned that they would all want to be part of Susan's funeral—the first of many signs of how much she meant to so many. The rector said Saturday at eleven o'clock would work for the service. I checked back with our various family members, and by the end of the day this was set.

Meanwhile, Andrew had appeared at the doorway. "You've already heard the news," I said to him, but he hadn't; he was just coming to visit Susan.

My colleague Michael told me of an undertaker he was satisfied with, and when I agreed, he called him and made preliminary arrangements.

The intern returned to see if I wanted an autopsy. All I could think was that Susan's body had suffered enough. I asked if there was anything that could be learned from an autopsy that might help someone else. No, he said; "it might answer questions for you, that's all." Well, she was dead, and I didn't need any more possible medical answers. I had spent more than nineteen years trying to solve Susan's medical problems; it was enough. "Let's let her body be," I said.

Dr. Wolf and his assistant arrived. They sat with me in the room for quite a while, asking about Susan, asking about me, asking about us. They gave me a chance to talk about important things that were nonmedical. I told them about my book on authority, and that I hoped to write some more about authority in practice. One chapter would be on the authority of a doctor. They encouraged me to contact them again.

Various doctors did what needed to be done. Her PEG tube wouldn't come out; finally they just cut it off close to her skin and put a Band-Aid on it. "A plaster," I thought.

It was important to me that her body be respected. I stayed with her through everything that was done: the washing, the wrapping in a clean sheet, the band around the head.

At some point, four of us—David, Michael, Andrew, and I—were standing around her flat bed, two on each side. I was from time to time touching her arm, stroking her cheek. I asked them for memories. It all felt at once calm and sacred.

By one thirty I was ready to leave the hospital, and David was to walk with me back to my apartment. Michael stayed, saying he wanted to remain with the body until people arrived to take it. I prayed a final blessing over Susan, asking that everyone into whose hands her body would now pass would treat her with reverence and loving care.

I managed that afternoon to write my final exam. I also wrote letters to my students and asked Joel to give them their letters only at the end, so that they would understand why I was absent but also would not be distracted by the news before taking the exam.

Emily arrived from Boston, driven down by two friends. Lots more phone calls were made as travel arrangements and sleeping arrangements were worked out. The Meads opened their apartment to my sisters-in-law. My colleague Michael and his wife opened theirs to my brother and his family. My parents, Emily, and Michael, who flew out with his daughter Lucy, would stay with me.

A Christian Service

Throughout her life Susan had taken to herself the wisdom of the church, and she was entrusted to that wisdom to the end. About three, maybe four hundred people attended her funeral. There were two bishops. There was a representative from the cardinal of New York. There were train cars full of people who came down from Dutchess County, where we had lived so long, people who knew Susan back when her tumor was found. There were thirty or forty boys who had often shared their refectory with her, who now sang for her the great music of the church. There were therapists and friends from the city who had helped Susan but never known her in the pretumor days. And there were hundreds of parishioners.

I knelt in the front row between Michael and Emily. With us was Lucy, not yet four years old, understanding somehow that Grandma had gone to be with Jesus. Lucy watched John Scott conduct the choir, and standing on the kneeler she waved her arm in imitation of his. Later, when we were kneeling for the eucharistic prayer, she stood between Michael and me, reaching her right arm around my neck and her left arm around his. What did she intuitively know, this little child? Or should I say, what did she not know?

At the end of the requiem mass, the ministers gather around the body. Prayers are said. The choir sings, "Give rest, O Christ, to thy servant with thy saints, where sorrow and pain are no more, neither sighing, but life everlasting." As they sing, I step into the aisle and receive the bucket of holy water and the aspergillum from the acolyte, and walk around the casket, casting holy water upon it.

And then it is time to go. The choir sings "In paradisum" as the ministers lead the body out. Michael and Emily and I follow immediately behind, and the rest of the family follows us. I grip the hand of each of them as we walk. It is a long aisle, and then we go out, down the steps to the car, where the body slides into place and is secured, and the car drives away.

Little Lady

What follows is the sermon that the Reverend Andrew C. Mead, rector of Saint Thomas Church, preached at the requiem for Susan Austin on December 22, 2012. Although it embarrasses me a bit at the end, I give it to the reader unexpurgated.

In the Name of God the Father, God the Son, and God the Holy Ghost. Amen.

I have known Susan since 2005, the year Victor accepted my call for him to come be our theologian-in-residence. At the time he and I talked considerably about what a move from a small college town to New York City—living in an apartment in the choir school—would mean for Susan and for the Saint Thomas community. I knew well that Victor would bless us richly with his teaching ministry. I did not know how much that blessing would involve Susan herself.

"She's on a long, slowly declining plateau," Victor said at the time. I never knew the brilliant, charming, witty soul Susan was at full strength before cancer struck her brain nearly twenty years ago, when the whole family was young. Victor and she had been sweethearts in college, but half of their marriage has been a valiant pilgrimage through slowly advancing disease and weakness. Yet even as her capacities were diminished, the cognitive brilliance, the wit and charm still shined. "Hey little lady," a homeless man called out to her on the street, and Susan would stop, nod, smile, turn towards and look at him; that was perhaps the best I-and-thou relationship that man might have that day. People in the parish helped Susan get to church, which she loved—all of it. She was still attending Victor's classes this fall before her last and final bout with the disease. I loved to kiss her on the cheek when I saw her, because she returned the sweetest smile and twinkling eyes. She read books. She gave presents. She wrote poetry and other things, almost to the very end.

She was a lioness—powerful even in weakness as a wife, mother of Emily and Michael, and grandmother of Lucy and James. She had always been a defender—including in clear, brisk prose—of the sanctity of human life at all stages and conditions, especially God's little ones: the poor, the sick, the unborn, the children (fostering crack babies), the old, the handicapped, the outcast; that is, she was a respecter of the dignity of every human being, as we say in Holy Baptism. The dignity of every human being consists in our being created and redeemed in the image of God. The image of God consists of our capacity to think, to choose, and to love (to make a sincere gift of oneself). At the heart of all this is our God-given freedom of the will, a capacity which Susan exercised, often with gusto and yes sometimes with willfulness, nearly to the end. A little vignette: Not too long ago, a parishioner who has helped the Austins noticed Susan seemed to be in a mood. Victor was there as well. The friend asked Susan if something was bothering her. "Yes!" she whispered loudly. "What's the matter?" he asked. She whispered even more emphatically, "Victor!" It's been a good marriage, all the way.

Susan and Victor had views about funeral sermons. They agreed the sermon should be about Jesus. Although this is the first time I have said the Lord's human name, he has been the subject all along: loyalty in a family; attention to all God's children, one by one; defender of the weak; vigorous exercise of faith and freedom; walking the way of the cross with courage and patience. It is all Jesus here.

There were two other things, two only, that they asked for. One was that her body be present before cremation. The form of the body is an important thing at a funeral, because it reminds us that neither in this life nor in the next are we disembodied souls—we are the union of body, soul, and spirit, on this side of death burdened by the inheritance of sin and death; on the other side of death the soul rests in peace waiting to be re-clothed with a glorious resurrection body. That glory can be seen in the Easter Gospels describing Jesus' own resurrection, the first fruits of those who have fallen asleep. I look forward, should God grant me this final gift of a heavenly resurrection, to seeing Susan in this glorious and resplendent state, a state of which her youthful brilliance is but a foretaste.

The other thing Susan and Victor asked for were hymns. Victor asked for "The strife is o'er, the battle done." Susan made Victor and the children memorize "He who would valiant be 'gainst all disaster" for the family's first and Susan's only trip to England. What better words for the pilgrimage of life? And who has walked it with more faith and love for Jesus than Susan and Victor alongside her? How much she has taught their children! And how much she has taught us all! Saint Thomas is so much richer in our communion and fellowship because of her. And what a tribute we see here before us. This mass, the music and ceremonial, the bishops, this congregation—we all want to offer this gift of love. "Hey little lady!" Our Susie has finished her pilgrimage on earth, and now Jesus has her entirely—she has crossed to him in safety. And Victor, we're here because of you, her faithful husband and our splendid priest. We love you and thank God for you. Our pilgrim's progress continues.

In the Name of God the Father, God the Son, and God the Holy Ghost. Amen.

Why Have You Forsaken Me?

Let us go then, you and I, to a cross on a hill. We have seen death; we must take courage and go see Death.

It has been dark since noon, a strange darkness that has blanketed the whole land and has lasted now for three hours. The biblical meaning of darkness is that God is displeased. There was darkness over the land of Egypt for three days, darkness so thick that it could be felt and the Egyptians could not even see one another: that was the penultimate plague that God sent to get the Egyptians to set free the Israelites; darkness was the penultimate plague, followed by the final plague in which every firstborn throughout the land died. Here at the cross we have darkness sent by God not for three days but for three hours, the penultimate dreadful sign to be followed by the final sign, the death of the Son.

Darkness was also to mark, according to the warnings of the Old Testament prophets, "the day of the Lord," a day of wrath, of punishment, of gloom. "The day of the LORD cometh," Joel said, "it is nigh at hand; a day of darkness and of gloominess, a day of clouds and of thick darkness" (2:1–2). Now that day has come, and it has come upon Jesus.

According to the Gospels of Matthew and Mark, nothing good happens to Jesus once he is put on the cross. All the signs are against him. He has been mocked, and his mockers have asked for a sign that he is the Son of God. Well, the sign has been given. Here is the sign that Jesus is the Son of God: darkness. God has pulled back.

Reader, do not miss the point. Everything turns against Jesus: the cosmos, the political world, his compatriots, his fellow religionists, his chosen companions, nature itself. There is no mercy. There is no grace. There is not even a fragrant breeze.

And have you ever thought about this? There is no silence.

One might hope to come to one's death in peace, to have a calmness and quiet about you within which you could compose yourself to face your end. Jesus had no peace. Not only did he have the pain from the nails and the agony of suffocation; he had the horror of screams. A crucifixion scene is a scene of screaming. Raymond Brown says that crucifixions were "particularly gruesome" because of "the screams of rage and pain, the wild curses and the outbreaks of nameless despair of the unhappy victims."

There was screaming around Jesus for hours from the others, only a fragment of which is recorded in the Gospels (their taunting of Jesus). And finally, at the end, Jesus himself screamed.

Yes, Jesus screamed out in the midst of his pain, not in rage, not in a curse, but in a loud cry. The Word of God incarnate does not merely speak; it is a screamed-out question, and it is his death cry. *My God, my God, why hast thou forsaken me?* What does it mean?

It means, I think, the obvious thing: that Jesus died in the worst way possible, that he died in unimaginable pain, and that his physical pain was accompanied by the mental and emotional pain of being abandoned by God. He entered into our human condition; he came down from heaven and was begotten by the Holy Ghost of the Virgin Mary and was made man. And then he went down further. He entered into the saddest and lowest human conditions; he entered into griefs and degradations and betrayals and tortures. He entered into them, he went down, and then he went down further. Jesus plumbed the absolute and literal depths of what it is to be human. He wept, sometimes with us and sometimes over us. He visited our tombs. And—it sounds trite but it's literally true—he shared our pain.

This, to be honest, is good news for us. There are no depths to which we may have to descend that Jesus has not already descended. However bad your life gets, Jesus will be with you. He can be with you, because he has gone down even further.

There is a profoundly moral novel by Jeffrey Eugenides called *The Marriage Plot.* The main character in it, at some point in his early twenties, goes to India. He wants to help in the work with Mother Teresa with the poorest of the poor; he wants, shall we say, to go down much further than he has had to go as a rather privileged Western college student. He is there for a couple of weeks, living with other volunteers, helping out on the sides and edges of things. One morning he is faced with a man who has massively defecated in his bed. In the midst of the chaos and the immense needs all around him, our young man suddenly cannot stand it.

Knowing he would regret it the rest of his life, he turns away from the wretch he should take care of, runs out of the building, scoops up his belongings, and escapes by train. The reader may regret the loss of a romantic image of personal growth and human fulfillment derived from charitable actions helping another human being, but actually, in my judgment, the novelist here demonstrates wisdom. Our character fell upon something true but awful about himself, that there were things he could not stand, depths into which he could not go. He discovered his limits, his frailty, his own fragility.

I understand this. In the years that I was the principal caregiver for Susan, I learned that there were caregiving things that I could do that I might otherwise never have thought to be within my capabilities. It was often humbling. My wife died, however, before I was tested in greater ways, and I do not know for sure how I would have been able to respond. I suspect, dear reader, that you know this same thing yourself. Perhaps through caring for someone you love, you have found that you are able to go a lot further down into the world of sickness and pain than you ever imagined you could. And yet all of us know that we have untested limits.

For Jesus there were no untested limits. And with trembling in our bones we can voice the sacred truth, that it is . . . good . . . that Jesus was so completely tested. For when Jesus screamed, it was, as I said, not in rage, not in anger, but in: a prayer. Although screamed out, the words *My God, my God, why hast thou forsaken me?* are a prayer. Jesus feels nothing but abandonment from God, and yet nonetheless he prays to God. He no longer feels any intimacy with God—less than twenty-four hours earlier he was praying to his "Father" that he be spared all this; now he cannot pray to his Father, but he can still pray like any human being can pray, to "God," to indeed "my God." He screams, yes, he cries out, yes, but it is a question that he cries, and a question rests upon a relationship, on the reality of one to whom a question is addressed. Jesus goes all the way down to the very bottom of human existence, and even at the bottom, even in the midst of all the pain of the universe, even in the absence of any sign at all that he has a divine Father, even there at the bottom a human being can still pray to God, can still ask, if nothing else, why this God, to whom he is speaking, why this God has forsaken him.

We find God by going down this road, down the road that goes down. Leonard Cohen, in his song "Suzanne" (which Susan used to sing to me), saw deeply, if not perfectly, when he said Jesus realized "only drowning men could see him." Jesus saw this from the cross (I think this is what Cohen means by "his lonely wooden tower"), where, Cohen says, he was "forsaken, almost human."

No, that last modifier is wrong: forsaken, *fully* human is the point. Yet it may be true that only drowning people can see Jesus. We who have suffered the depths can catch sight of him, I think, because Jesus was fully human all the way down: in the darkness, beyond the darkness, forsaken, fully human, he sank (as Cohen almost says) beneath God's wisdom like a stone.

Divergence and a Dream

The day following Susan's requiem was the Fourth Sunday of Advent. I took comfort in being a priest and having something to do, and my colleagues allowed me to participate as much as I wanted. While I was walking to church that cool, bright December morning, a vision of sorts came to me. It was the strong sense that Susan had gone off on a very exciting journey. Like a C. S. Lewis story—perhaps like the end of *The Last Battle*, when the cry is heard, "Come further up, come further in!"—Susan had gone up, off, somewhere, a place at whose existence all her beloved stories had hinted. No longer merely a story, now it was true for her; it was reality; it was adventure.

But it was also clear: not for me that journey, not now. I was heading in a new direction. What would it be? As I write these words, it is still not clear to me what my direction is to be. But God has vouchsafed me two unmistakable messages.

The first was obvious. No longer would I be taking care of Susan. The time I had given to her now would be given back to me and would be available for other purposes. I imagined I might write a lot more, and I imagined other, more fanciful things. To be honest, I used a lot of my "extra" time those first months just sleeping. Unless I had an appointment, I didn't worry about when I got up. I did the work I had to do. I spent time with friends. I taught classes at church and, the next fall, at Fordham again. I went to conferences. But all this was undertaken only as it came to me and not through my design. I have been waiting on God to make clear in his good time what he has for me to do. This book is, in fact, the first major work of my post-Susan days.

At once, I say, the obvious fact was clear to me that I would no longer need to take care of Susan. Then a couple of weeks later, the other shoe dropped. I realized she no longer needed me.

This came to my psyche as a hard lesson. For nearly twenty years, the most important things I had done had been connected with the care of Susan. I had taken charge, of necessity, of increasingly larger aspects of her life. She had needed me. But it is hard when caregiving to remember that *the recipient of one's care is one's equal*. As I've related in this book, I often hated the bind that I was in. Well, now I was out of the bind, and was I willing to recognize that Susan had become again what she always was, my equal? For in truth that is the case. She has passed out of my care into the hands of Jesus, who is doing for her better things than I can ask or imagine. Yes, I know that! But can I accept that this means we are once again peers in the sight of God, able to stand with equal integrity side by side—even though she is no longer within my visible sight?

And so we come to the second message. Two or three months after her death, I had the first dream in which Susan figured. We were in a place—sort of an unknown neighborhood—an Argo Tea shop was there, and there was a children's school with an unusual name I can't remember. In the dream, it was an unspoken given that this school was a great one for young children. Susan and I walked into the school, where she and someone else were taken farther down the hall, and I stayed with a man in a rather dull and cluttered medium-sized room with white walls. He showed me a vacuum cleaner while sitting at his computer desk. Someone arrived with a child at the door of the room, and I felt I was in the way, so I told him to go on, I could figure it out myself. I gathered in my arms the vacuum cleaner and a computer terminal and awkwardly carried them down the hall and found Susan. Still with someone else, she was sitting in something like an open café booth, but it wasn't a food place; it was still the same place. She said that someone in the next room wanted to talk to me. It was a reception desk such as one finds in a doctor's office. Two young women were there, and one of them told me they wanted to give Susan a job application for, I realized afterwards, a job at this remarkable school. I took the application to Susan and thought, well, they'll see she can't fill this out by herself. But she started doing so. And I awoke.

The dream's meaning is rather obvious. I was involved with things like cleaning and computer work, while Susan had gone on down the hall to a future life. Then it hit me: she was able to fill in the application herself. How many times over the past twenty years had we visited doctors' offices, been given paperwork, and I had been the one to fill it out because Susan couldn't? And now she can.

When I stood beside her still-warm body in the hospital room with my friends gathered around, I knew at once that she was now in Jesus' hands and—it has become a mantra for me—he was, and still is, doing better things for her than I could ask or imagine. What are those things? By definition, as it were, they are things that I cannot imagine.

I do not know if Susan is aware of me now. There is no rea-son to think she is, and no reason to deny it either. What is the relationship in time and space of this life to those whom Jesus is taking care of, as, I believe, he is taking care of Susan? Is her "time" in sync with ours? Does it intersect at all? Does she even have awareness "now"?

The Christian faith holds that there is life after death, and then, in N. T. Wright's wonderful phrase, there is "life after life after death." That is to say, there is "a yet more glorious day" ahead of us, ahead of all of us, ahead of you who read this book and ahead of those, like Susan, who have died—a yet more glorious day of resurrection, when there is given to all the redeemed an illustrious body that will never grow old, never lose its hair, never hunger, never suffer cancer or chemotherapy or loss of memory or brain seizures, a body that is completely alive in God's Holy Spirit, which is what is meant when we say "a spiritual body": this is ahead for both Susan and me, I pray, and for you, may we pray. Susan's journey has diverged from mine, but at the end we will converge, God willing, with all the saints.

And then, if the likes of C. S. Lewis and Susan Austin are right, the real action will begin.

Epilogue

To Plumb the Depths of God's Love

BY SUSAN AUSTIN

After God made the world, he took his little servant, man, and taught him to pray like this: "Bow your head," said God, "and say 'Lord, have mercy,' and then you will do what is right." Similarly he taught his little servants the animals to pray: "Be faithful to your own," said God, "keep your families, and sing the songs I have taught you, and then you will do what is right." But to the trees he taught no prayer.

"What about us, Lord?" they asked him. "Teach us to pray like the others." But God said, "Wait, little friends. I don't yet know what to teach you." Then he went back to heaven and rested for

Among Susan's papers is this little story, written in her small hand on just a sheet and a half of unlined yellow paper. There is no indication of the date nor of any attempt to get the story published; I would place it in the decade or so before her tumor was discovered, but that is only a guess. I have supplied the title.

three days from his worries. He sent Michael the Archangel to watch over things in his absence, and commanded him to report back every day on the state of things.

The first day Michael came back and said: "The men are praying the way you taught them." "Yes, I hear them," said God. "They are faithful servants to me." So Michael went back to earth.

The second day he came into God's presence and said: "The animals are praying the way you taught them." God said, "I hear them—they are my faithful servants." So Michael went back to earth.

The third day he came into heaven and said: "O God forever blessed! Some of your servants are sorrowing." God said, "How can that be, Michael? I don't hear any cries." "O God forever blessed!" said Michael. "Your trees are grieving because you never taught them how to pray. They are mourning, and in their great sorrow they are tearing off their leaves and scattering them on the ground." At those words God remembered that he had not taught them, and he took pity on his faithful servants.

He descended down to earth and walked among them. At first they never saw him because of the great burden of their sorrow; they tore off their leaves and strewed them on him as he walked under their branches. At last God himself wept in his mercy and made himself known to them.

"O trees, my little friends," he said, "stop tearing off your leaves and scattering them about but listen to me. Listen carefully, because I have thought of a prayer for you to pray."

Instantly the trees stopped their lamentations and composed themselves to listen. "Hear me then, trees," said God. "This is the way you must pray: not with words nor with songs, but with silence, and branches lifted in supplication. Don't be afraid that I won't hear you. I have ears to hear the most silent heart and I love to pour myself out in the quietness. Only keep your branches forever raised in prayer, and I will not forget you."

"O King, be praised forever," said the trees in their joy, and with one accord they raised their branches up in supplication to heaven, and fell into a deep silence. So God went back up to his throne and listened with love to the prayers of all his faithful servants.

Now it happened that the world fell into misery and death; and God, to defeat death, sent his own beloved Son to die. The way that it was arranged for him to perish was by hanging on the wood of a tree, and at this the trees were aghast.

"Lord," they said in the stillness of their hearts, "didn't we cradle him when he was a child?" "You did," said God, remembering. "Also," they said, "didn't we give a livelihood to his father so he could eat?" "You did," said God, remembering. "Didn't we form the boat from which he taught the crowds?" "All this is true," said God. "Then, O!" they mourned, "why must he suffer on us, why must our hard, stiff nature be the thing on which he breaks himself and dies? Why have you appointed us to treat the Beloved so bitterly?" God looked at the trees most tenderly and said, "My dear ones, you have not yet plumbed the depths of my love."

But they did not believe him and when God's Son had died and light was extinguished out of the world, with one accord they dropped their branches and tore off their leaves in mourning.

"The Son is dead," they wailed, "and we have killed him! He died to save us but we did not save him! He is gone and joy is gone forever!" Likewise so wailed all the animals and men.

And God also wept on his throne in heaven.

But after he had done weeping, he plumbed the depths of his love and at the very heart and deepest place of his love he found the dead Son and this Son he brought back into the light of day. This happened early in the morning.

Now God's Son was walking about in a garden and the silent trees saw him. An awe stole over them, though they did not recognize him: but slowly, slowly they lifted their bare, ragged branches up towards heaven: and the dawn began to break.

And slowly, slowly a new sap ascended through all their veins and capillaries, and they began to wonder if they understood the extent of God's love. And the Man walking in the garden reminded them a little of God's Son: and the sky turned pink and gold:

And just as the sun rose, they recognized their Beloved and saw that he was alive, and with one accord they burst into flower, and the scent of those flowers rose straight to the throne of God.

Thus God taught them to pray twice: once at the very beginning of the world, and once when he gave them a new prayer to pray after they had plumbed the depths of his love.

Notes

Scripture quotations from the Song of Songs are taken from the Revised English Bible © 1989 Oxford University Press and Cambridge University Press.

Scripture quotations from Job (unless marked "Sacks") are taken from the Revised Standard Version of the Bible, copyright 1952 [2nd ed., 1971] by the Division of Christian Education of the National Council of the Churches of Christ in the United States of America. Used by permission. All rights reserved.

Scripture quotations from the Psalms are taken from the 1979 (U.S.) Book of Common Prayer.

Other unattributed Scripture quotations are from the Authorized (King James) Version of the Bible.

Susan Austin's article "The Aborting Community" was published in *The Human Life Review* 8, no. 4 (Fall 1982): 55–62; repr., 38, no. 1 (Winter 2012): 54–60. The selections quoted herein are reprinted by kind permission of the publisher.

"Prayer No Longer Makes Sense" has been revised from a section of Victor Lee Austin, *A Priest's Journal* (New York: Church Publishing, 2001).

"Prevenient Grace" and "Susan Walking" have been revised from sections of Victor Lee Austin, *Priest in New York: Church, Street, and Theology* (New York: Saint Thomas Church, 2010).

William F. Buckley Jr.'s letter to Susan is published here by kind permission of his son, Christopher F. Buckley.

Father Mead's sermon "Little Lady" is published here by his kind permission.

The Prufrock quote is from T. S. Eliot, "The Love Song of J. Alfred Prufrock," the seventh line from the end. The first line of the section "Why Have You Forsaken Me?" is also from this poem, its first line. And it is in "East Coker," part 4, that Eliot says we will "Die" of God's care. Both poems can be found in T. S. Eliot, *The Complete Poems and Plays, 1909–1950* (New York: Harcourt, Brace & World, 1962).

When our children were reading "The world is charged with the grandeur of God" to Susan, they had in their hands one of my first gifts to her: *Poems of Gerard Manley Hopkins*, 4th ed., ed. W. H. Gardner and N. H. MacKenzie (London: Oxford University Press, 1967).

For the discussion of the second-best book in the Bible, I have drawn upon Robert W. Jenson, *Song of Songs* (Louisville: John Knox, 2005). The direct quotation is from p. 54.

Brian Davies writes about the oddness of God and the nonsense it is to speak of God as "morally well-behaved" in many of his books. See, for instance, *The Reality of God and the Problem of Evil* (London: Continuum, 2006) and *Thomas Aquinas on God and Evil* (New York: Oxford University Press, 2011).

My discussion of the best book in the Bible is guided by the remarkable commentary by Robert Sacks, a tutor at St. John's College in Santa Fe who, perhaps coincidentally, was an intellectual influence on Susan. This commentary with an original translation exists in different versions, both in the journal *Interpretation* and as a printed book. I quote from Robert D. Sacks, *The Book of Job: Translations and Musings* (bound photocopy, 1993). The quotation from Job marked "Sacks" is from this volume.

My understanding of Jesus' cry from the cross has been informed by the magisterial two-volume work of Raymond E. Brown, *The Death of the Messiah* (New York: Doubleday, 1994). The quotation about screaming is from vol. 2, p. 1044.

Acknowledgments

The Reverend Andrew C. Mead encouraged me to write about Susan, saying something ridiculous about me being able to do what C. S. Lewis did in *A Grief Observed*. But he was wise to prod me to do this, wise to encourage me to go deep and be honest. And for his trust and friendship I am grateful beyond telling.

Before I had written a line of this book, I posed the thought of it to David Nelson of Brazos Press. He was immediately taken with the project and has supported and challenged me through its gestation.

I importuned a number of my theological colleagues and friends to read this manuscript. Stanley Hauerwas, Stephen Hildebrand, Robert Jenson, and Tobias Winright all gave generously of their time and advice; may our friendships continue to deepen. My children also have read this book and allowed me to go forward into deep places even at emotional cost to them. Emily took precious time away from her own dissertation writing in order to give me extensive notes on particular sections, putting me in that wonderfully paradoxical place of a parent who finds his child has become his peer.

A complete set of acknowledgments would include my son and daughter-in-law, whose heart-to-heart conversations have nourished me, and their children (now four, of whom Susan met only two), with whom I've shared a plenitude of hugs, hugs whose meaning is beyond their present understanding; my parents, who embraced Susan as their own daughter; Susan's sisters, who look out for me; widows and widowers with whom I have had pastoral conversations, both in my parish and among my priestly colleagues; future brides and grooms who have thought with me, during premarital counseling sessions, about "for better for worse"; my Fordham students, who want to know what true friendship is; my colleagues Joel and Charles, whose own losses early in their lives silently undergird our friendships; my colleague Michael, who, when I told him I had taken off my wedding ring on Christmas Eve, said so lovingly, "How does that feel?" Well, it feels both right and wrong: I still reach with my thumb to the base of that finger, trying to rub the ring that is no longer there. . . . And so many more. Indeed, were I to acknowledge everyone who has had an influence on this book, I think I would need to name everyone in my life.